FIONA DOYLE

Fiona Doyle is a playwright whose work in theatre includes *Coolatully* (winner of the 2014 Papatango New Writing Prize) at the Finborough Theatre in London, and for Mead Theatre Lab in Washington DC; *Deluge* (winner of the 2014 Eamon Keane Full-length Play Award) at Hampstead Theatre Downstairs; *The Annihilation of Jessie Leadbeater* (ALRA); *The Ceasefire Babies* (NT Connections); and *Abigail* (The Bunker Theatre). Her short plays include *Rootbound* and *Rigor Mortis* (Arcola Theatre) and *Ms Y* (Young Vic). She is the recipient of the Irish Theatre Institute's inaugural Phelim Donlon Playwright's Bursary and Residency Award in association with the Tyrone Guthrie Centre, a fellowship from the MacDowell Colony in New Hampshire and an attachment to the National Theatre Studio.

Other Titles in this Series

Fiona Doyle

THE STRANGE
DEATH OF
JOHN DOE

NICK HERN BOOKS

London

www.nickhernbooks.co.uk

A Nick Hern Book

The Strange Death of John Doe first published in Great Britain in 2018 as a paperback original by Nick Hern Books Limited, The Glasshouse, 49a Goldhawk Road, London W12 8QP

Designed and typeset by Nick Hern Books, London
Printed in the UK by Mimeo Ltd, Huntingdon, Cambridgeshire PE29 6XX

A CIP catalogue record for this book is available from the British Library

ISBN 978 1 84842 767 9

Woodland CARBON
www.woodlandcarbon.co.uk
NICK HERN BOOKS
Printed on Carbon Captured paper

The Strange Death of John Doe was first performed at
Hampstead Theatre Downstairs, London, on 25 May 2018.
The cast was as follows:

FELIPE/AIRPORT SECURITY/ AVIATION OFFICIAL	Damola Adelaja
GER	Charlotte Bradley
XIMO	Benjamin Cawley
ANNA/RAE	Callie Cooke
THE DOCUMENT DOCTOR/ PAULINO/MORUF	Maynard Eziashi
SAMUEL/JAN/TRAVELLER/ CORONER	Nick Hendrix
JOHN KAVURA	Rhashan Stone
CARTER	Abigail Thaw

Director	Edward Hall
Designer	Michael Pavelka
Movement developed by	Scott Ambler
Lighting	Matthew Haskins
Sound	Chris Murray

'Tell me, what is it you plan to do
with your one wild and precious life?'

Mary Oliver

Acknowledgements

This play has been on a long journey and has had the support of a great number of people along the way; to each and every one of them – thank you:

Rakie Ayola
Peter Bankolé
Paige Carter
Mark Extance
Franc Ashman
Ashley Zhangazha
Babou Ceesay
Mairead McKinley
Rebecca Humphries
Leah Whitaker
Sean Delaney
Jason Barnett
Oliver Dimsdale
Kate Maravan
Danny Lee Wynter
Gunnar Cauthery
Jude Akuwudike
Issy van Randwyck
Damola Adelaja
Charlotte Bradley
Benjamin Cawley
Callie Cooke
Maynard Eziashi
Nick Hendrix
Rhashan Stone
Abigail Thaw
Anna Girvan
Andy Smart
Rob Chapman
Cassie Lane
Clare Broom
Ellie Mercala
Takayasu Ogura

Oliver Reed
Richard Bond
Chris Delderfield
Ian Butler
Juliette Franklin
Mike White
Chris Murray
Matt Haskins
Michael Pavelka
Lucia Benadikova
Katie Pesskin
Sally C Roy
Beth Absalom
Simon Slater
Will Mortimer
Greg Ripley-Duggan
Hampstead Theatre
Tom Lyons
Matthew Poxon
The National Theatre Studio
The Susan Smith Blackburn Prize
Camilla Young
Eileen Doyle
Greg Marshall
Lucas Schaefer
Amy Gall
John Burgess
Roy Williams
Jocelyn Abbey
Tom Carney

And thank you in particular to the following two people:

Scott Ambler, who left his indelible mark on our final draft and whose presence was greatly missed in the rehearsal room.

And Ed Hall, for believing so much in this play and in me. I am forever indebted to him.

F.D.

For Jose.
And all the others.

Characters

XIMO, *late twenties, Mozambican. 'Ximo' is a pet name. Short for Joaquim. Pronounced 'ZEE–MO'*

FELIPE, *late twenties/early thirties, Mozambican. Ximo's older brother. A fireball of energy*

GER, *mid-fifties, Irish. Consultant Forensic Pathologist*

ANNA, *mid-twenties, English. Trainee Anatomical Pathology Technician*

SAMUEL, *mid-twenties. Trainee Anatomical Pathology Technician*

RAE, *late twenties/early thirties. South African and German citizenship*

CARTER, *late thirties, Detective Chief Inspector with the Metropolitan Police*

JOHN KAVURA, *thirties, Detective Sergeant with the Metropolitan Police*

THE DOCUMENT DOCTOR, *late forties, Mozambican police official*

AIRPORT SECURITY MAN, *thirties. Angolan*

JAN, *married to Rae. White South African. Mafia*

MORUF, *Nigerian, late forties. A 'voluntary returnee'*

PAULINO, *Mozambican. Speaks fluent English*

TRAVELLER

AVIATION OFFICIAL

CORONER

This text went to press before the end of rehearsals and so may differ slightly from the play as performed.

Note on Text

(/) marks the point where the immediately following dialogue or action overlaps.

(–) marks the point at which a sentence is cut off abruptly by the speaker themselves or by something or someone else.

(…) suggests a thought changing track; a hesitation; a loss for words.

In this play, the morgue is at the centre of everything. It must maintain a permanent presence. Sometimes we are solely focused on the mortuary; sometimes there are other scenes happening around it, through it, in front of it, but we must always be aware of its existence, right until the very end. Ger controls the radio and her preferred station is Classic FM.

Movement, transitions and sound are as important as the dialogue. Use these moments. The different worlds of the play should feel separate and yet connected. At certain points they pass close by each other; sometimes they directly collide. Numerous strangers gradually brought together by the death of one man; like threading beads on a piece of string.

It's best that the set is as pared down as possible and as many props as possible come from the mortuary. For example, Ger's hedge shears for cutting ribs become Ximo's hedge shears in the garden in Cape Town. Or a vessel for collecting bodily fluids might become John's whiskey glass in the bar, etc. The original production also benefited from the multifunctional use of the gurneys or body trays. For instance, a gurney might suddenly become a table in Carter's office; or the perimeter fence of the Quatro de Fevereiro Airport might be created by raising the side rails on numerous gurneys; or placed end-to-end, they might become the cramped wheel-well space that Ximo has to crawl through and so on.

Depending on how individual companies approach transitions, there doesn't always have to be a physical body on the gurney; sometimes an imaginary body might be implied.

Often, Ximo is observing his own autopsy. Sometimes he even assists with transitions; for example, handing props to other actors when they're about to play out a scene from his past, in a bid to ensure that the truth of his story continues to unfold.

In the original production, a chorus of morticians was used to great effect. The only actor who was never part of this chorus was the actor playing Ximo. They used screens to 'magically' reveal other characters while cleverly disguising scene transitions. At certain points they became revellers in a busy Maputo nightclub or dancers in the Document Doctor's bar. Sometimes they simply watched scenes play out and sometimes they helped 'instruct' Ximo by, say, tapping on a gurney to let him know that it was time to lie back down. They always wore half-masks and their stylised presence helped create an appropriate sense of the surreal and different worlds colliding.

Anna and Sam are hugely competitive with each other.

In the original production, the actor playing Anna also doubled as Rae, which worked very effectively.

In the original production, Ximo's first monologue (p. 17) was also broken up and repeated at various points in the play. Some of it was used as 'time passes' in the mortuary, or mixed in with the radio static, for example. Fragments were woven through the play in an attempt to keep Ximo's voice ever-present (and the voicemails at the top of the play might also be used in a similar manner).

Lastly, this play should at times feel a bit like a dream inside a dead man's head.

Total darkness.

Sound of a phone ringing from far away. And jet engines firing up.

The shape of something crawling starts to emerge. A person.

We also hear the voice of the AIRPORT SECURITY MAN *giving instructions:*

'From the bar, haul yourself up into the well and move along the side until you come to a small opening. Crawl through that opening and it will lead you out into the landing-gear retract area. Tuck your legs up like so and stay there. Got it? Otherwise you might get crushed.'

Mechanical noises now. The morticians start moving the gurneys around the person who is crawling, as if to suggest someone is deep inside the interior of a plane as it takes up position on a runway.

VOICEMAIL. The person you are trying to reach is unable to get to the phone. Please leave a message after the tone.

Tone.

FELIPE'S VOICE. Hey. Where are you? This isn't... I'd like to kick you up the ass right now! (*Beat.*) Are you there? Did you really go?

Another phone starts ringing. The voices start to overlap.

VOICEMAIL. / The person you are trying to reach is unable to answer the phone. Please leave a message after the tone.

FELIPE'S VOICE. Louis has a new car. It's a nice car. Took our first tour out three days ago. Four Americans and a German. They were all still alive by the end.

We can see XIMO *now. He's wearing a grey hoodie, jeans, and white trainers. He's on his hands and knees squeezing through a tiny space.*

Hey. I'm wearing your trousers. Right now. Without underwear! (*Beat.*) Always moving, eh? Always flitting about. Call me you little shit.

Tone.

RAE'S VOICE. Hi. It's me.

Everything suddenly stops. The entire focus should be on RAE*'s voice here.*

I thought you might have called by now. I don't want it to be like this. (*Beat.*) Maybe you've found a girl? Or a job? Or both? I can come visit. I can come visit you and you can introduce me to your girl. We can all go out for tea together. I never planned this y'know. Who gets to plan their life, hey?

As the voicemail continues, the mechanical noises start up again and the gurneys begin to close in on XIMO, *like something is retracting.* XIMO *starts to push against them, as if he has changed his mind suddenly but it's too late. They lock in tightly. He is cramped and uncomfortable. Trapped. He manages to kiss some prayer beads before putting them in his pocket.*

I never used you either. I never did that. I was just trying to help. (*Beat.*) It's been such a long time Ximo. Seems like a lifetime ago now. (*Beat.*) And maybe you were using me, ever thought about that? Wherever you are, I hope you're okay. (*Beat.*) God. Life just goes on doesn't it? Life just goes –

Line goes dead as the overwhelming sound of a jet plane taking off fills the auditorium. It's deafening. XIMO *covers his ears.*

Louder.

Louder.

Louder…

XIMO (*shouting over the roaring engines, as if someone has just asked him a question*). What does it feel like? Ringing. In my brain. First the right. Then the left. Then the right *and* the left until my head is filled with bells as clouds pass beneath my feet.

The engines level off a bit now, replaced by the steady hum of a plane flying at high altitude.

Dizzy. Strange shapes. Air is cold. Head feels light. Rushing forward, dropping back. Never knew it could turn cold like this. Pressure. In my heart, on my chest, get the fuck off my chest. Squeezing. Pressing. Crushing. No one told me I wouldn't be able to breathe. Rock on my heart. Stealing it away out over the sea. And black. Falling. Through a dark dark space. (*Laughs.*) So dramatic.

The sound of a wheel well opening. Then all mechanical noises cease. Now, we just hear space and wind.

Light comes back a moment as the ground beneath me appears. Dropping out into the world. Falling through space. And time. Into space and time. Falling. Until…

Teeth.
Face.
Phone.

The sound of a body smashing to pieces.

***

London. Monday morning in late September. An office in a police station.

CARTER. She wants want?

JOHN. Compensation.

CARTER. For what?

JOHN. Her flowerbeds.

CARTER. Her flowerbeds?

JOHN. Apparently they're quite rare. A speciality or something. Called – (*Reading from a notebook.*) Rose Alexander. (*Looks at CARTER.*) That's a hybrid tea rose, has a particular type of maintenance programme.

CARTER (*despairingly*). Jesus Christ.

JOHN. Saw some forget-me-nots growing by the wall. They're the little blue ones, y'know? We used have them out the back when I was a kid.

CARTER *looks at him, expecting more.*

What about the Angolans?

CARTER. Let's just say I get the feeling this isn't an investigation of great urgency for them.

JOHN. Is there no other way / of

CARTER. It *has* to be through the Angolan authorities.

Beat.

JOHN (*looking at notes*). Oh yeah, and she remembers hearing a car alarm going off briefly around 8.15 a.m.

CARTER. Hybrid-tea-rose lady?

JOHN. Yeah.

CARTER. She look outside?

JOHN. You know what people are like, I put a pillow over my head.

CARTER. 8.15. (*Beat.*) All matches up.

JOHN. I'll go ring pathology. See where they're at.

JOHN *goes to exit. He suddenly gets a vivid flashback of the body in the garden – the contortion, the blood, the utter annihilation of this unknown man.*

CARTER. John?

JOHN. Yeah?

CARTER. What time d'you get to bed last night?

JOHN. What?

CARTER. Your eyes look red.

JOHN. Allergies.

CARTER. What d'you do after your shift / last night?

JOHN. None of your bloody / business Carter.

CARTER. You can't keep this up.

JOHN *just looks at her.*

People are starting to notice.

Beat.

JOHN. I need to go ring pathology. Detective Chief Inspector.

They hold eye contact for a moment.

CARTER. Fine. Fine John. Go ring pathology.

JOHN *exits.* CARTER *picks up the phone.*

(*To herself as she dials.*) Fucking fuck.

A transition into the mortuary. GER *is making some notes on a clipboard to which a number of white identification tags are attached. She is dressed in disposable garments that cover her from head to toe – the gown is ankle-length, blue, surgical. She also wears a plastic apron, a tie-on surgical cap, shoe covers, etc. She rolls her shoulders, cracks her neck and tunes in her radio.* SAMUEL *enters. He is dressed almost identically,*

GER (*double-checking her notes*). Any sign of her?

SAMUEL. Not yet.

GER. Right. Well – (*Glances to an outside area, then looks at the clock.*) We should start. (*Looks at SAMUEL for a moment.*) Apron?

SAMUEL (*looking down*). Shit. Yeah. Sorry.

GER *rolls her eyes as he exits to get the apron. A phone starts ringing somewhere.*

GER (*filling out an identification tag*). And get that while yer at it.

ANNA *rushes in.*

You're late.

ANNA. I know, I know, I'm sorry.

GER. It's your observation session Anna –

ANNA (*pulling on her disposable garments as she speaks*). I know but this bloke came off his bike on the high street right in front of me. Couldn't just leave him there could I, so I go over to help an' he tells me to fuck off. Can you believe that? I'm trying to help him an' he just tells me to fuck off. Well anyway, I told him to fuck off right back. I mean what's wrong with people, y'know?

SAMUEL *re-enters.*

SAMUEL. You're late.

ANNA. Fuck off.

GER (*finishes last tag*). That them again?

SAMUEL. Yeah.

GER (*sighing*). We're going to have to prioritise number three.

ANNA. What's so special 'bout number three?

GER. Police need reconstruction shots and they won't stop bugging me 'til they get them – (*To* ANNA.) are you ready yet? (*To* SAMUEL.) Pull him out.

ANNA *hurriedly finishes putting on her gear.*

SAMUEL (*as he manoeuvres the gurney containing* XIMO'*s body out into the middle of the room*). Lucky number three, eh? Skipping the queue.

GER. Nothin' lucky about this number three.

A transition. XIMO *sits up and the* MORTICIANS *start helping him to remove the clothing he is wearing. The items are laid out on the gurney as if they now represent his body.* XIMO *stands back and observes. Perhaps we hear some of* XIMO'*s speech as this happens.*

ANNA *and* SAMUEL *are now going through the clothes of the deceased.*

SAMUEL (*examining a grey hoodie*). No bag or nothing. Just the clothes he was in. Crazy.

ANNA (*inspecting a pair of jeans*). Maybe it fell out somewhere along the way. (*Feeling along the lining of the pocket.*) I think there's… a tear in the lining…

XIMO *is watching her. Then reluctantly, he leans over and drops the SIM card in for* ANNA *to find. She holds it up.*

SIM card.

GER. See? What did I tell you. Police officers don't like searching dead bodies. Bag it up.

A moment where the SIM card becomes the focus of the entire room as it is bagged up. Perhaps this is done in slow motion.

ANNA. There's something else in here too.

XIMO *now produces a beaded necklace. He leans in and drops it into the pocket.* ANNA *pulls out the necklace and examines it.*

Some kind've… necklace or something.

GER. Bag it and note it.

The beads are sealed up in a clear plastic bag. SAMUEL *picks up a pen and clipboard.*

SAMUEL (*writing*). SIM card. Inside lining. Left pocket. Plus brown – (*To* ANNA.) what do I call it?

ANNA. Necklace.

SAMUEL. Plus brown. *Beaded.* Necklace.

ANNA. Pair've trainers. White.

SAMUEL (*writes*). White. Trainers. Make?

ANNA. Gola.

SAMUEL *writes.*

Red T-shirt, green stripes.

SAMUEL *writes.*

S'that rain?

SAMUEL. Size?

ANNA. What?

SAMUEL. T-shirt.

ANNA. Medium.

SAMUEL *writes.*

(*Trying to read brand name.*) Can you make that out? (*Shows the scuffed label to* GER.)

GER. No.

SAMUEL. Label. Illegible.

ANNA. Soiled with bodily fluids.

ANNA *places the T-shirt in a separate bag for disposal.*

SAMUEL (*writing*). Health hazard. High risk.

ANNA. Grey hoodie… Adidas…

GER. Real or fake?

ANNA. How can you tell?

GER. Let's have a look? (*Shows her the label.*) Fake. See those stitches?

XIMO *turns away suddenly and moves to another part of the room. As he does so, the lights flicker on and off. When he stops, they're normal again.*

GER. Keep meaning to get that looked at.

SAMUEL. Freaks me out when that happens.

They continue.

ANNA. Soiled with bodily fluids.

SAMUEL/ANNA. Health hazard.

ANNA. Blue jeans.

> SAMUEL *writes.*

> Medium.

> SAMUEL *writes.*

> No brand name.

> SAMUEL *writes.*

> That's it.

GER. Rings? Watch? Money?

ANNA. Nothing. (*Nodding to the SIM-card bag.*) Maybe there's something on that though. Maybe they'll be able to call someone.

GER. Maybe.

> *A transition as* XIMO *repositions himself on the body tray. As this is happening we hear…*

AIRPORT SECURITY MAN (*voice-over*). Now listen carefully. There's a breach in the fence about three hundred yards that way. It's tight but manageable. When you get through you need to follow the internal road to the international terminal, entendeu? 'Internacional.' You'll find a British Airways plane sitting on the tarmac. It leaves at midnight.

> *More time has passed.* ANNA *is now carrying out an external examination on the body.* SAMUEL *is noting down her observations while* GER *oversees everything. All three are wearing latex gloves and splash shields.*

ANNA. Streaks here too. See?

SAMUEL (*makes a note*). Oil marks. Lower. Abdomen.

ANNA. And some scars. Old ones I think. Back of his right hand.

SAMUEL. Old. Scars.

SAMUEL laughs to himself.

ANNA. What?

SAMUEL. D'you remember that bloke from last week? Fella with the nail polish on his little / finger?

GER. Samuel.

SAMUEL. Sorry.

He continues writing.

ANNA. Don't forget the tattoo.

SAMUEL. Butterfly tattoo. Left wrist.

GER. Right. I'll start you off. (*Selects a small knife and begins the autopsy.*) So. Making my incision from the neck down and meeting where?

ANNA/SAMUEL. Mid-chest.

ANNA (*to* SAMUEL). S'my observation session.

SAMUEL pulls a face at her. She pulls one straight back. GER makes the first cut.

GER. Then continue all the way down to the pubic area and… voilà. (*Nods at* ANNA.) All yours.

ANNA selects a cutting appliance that looks like a medium-sized hedge shear and starts cutting open the ribcage. We hear every bone break.

ANNA. Really… stiff, isn't it?

GER. Don't be afraid to use more force. Bones have to crack if you want to get in.

ANNA. Looks like he's seen something awful.

GER. Stop looking at his face and look at what you're doing.

ANNA keeps cutting but the body is stiff and resistant.

SAMUEL (*inspecting face*). Don't have a face left really, does he.

A phone rings somewhere.

GER (*to* SAMUEL). Get that, will you?

SAMUEL *flounces off, annoyed at having to play secretary today for the second time.*

ANNA. I'm sorry but... can you...

GER *gets a towel and gently covers the face.* ANNA *continues.*

GER. Nearly there now.

ANNA. Look like hedge shears.

GER. They are hedge shears. Do as good a job for half the price. But just make sure you don't leave them lying about during an inspection. (*Looking at her work.*) Like cutting through a branch.

ANNA *completes the job.*

Good woman.

SAMUEL *re-enters.*

SAMUEL. Police again. Want to know when he'll be ready –

GER. Right. Tell them to stop ringing us now 'cause we'll ring them. We'll fucking ring them when he's ready, won't we.

SAMUEL (*utterly used to* GER *flaring like this occasionally, no big deal*). Got it.

He exits. GER *composes herself.*

GER (*to* ANNA). Select your tools.

We hear SAMUEL *on the phone offstage, repeating exactly what* GER *just told him to say, as* ANNA *starts selecting and laying out her tools for removal of organs. Then we hear voices on the air as a transition takes place.*

What is that? Sorry, I... (*Laughter.*) *Who did you think it would be?*

I don't know.

Are you a nervous person?

No. Not usually.

I like your voice.

We are at the police station again. CARTER *has just popped in to* JOHN's *office and asked a question. The removal of organs happens as this scene plays out.*

JOHN. Came in over the weekend. Morgues don't do weekends.

CARTER. Right.

JOHN. Said they'll ring once he's ready.

CARTER. Okay.

JOHN. Said 'we'll fucking ring you when he's ready, won't we'.

Beat. CARTER *studies* JOHN *for a moment.*

CARTER. Fifteen other officers passed that exam too. They can't fast-track people.

JOHN. Sorry?

CARTER. To more senior positions. They can't do that –

JOHN. I know they can't bloody do that, that's not / what I'm

CARTER. Watch your tone there John, yeah? (*Beat.*) Top of the class when we graduated, remember? But Christ, you're unrecognisable now and they can see that John, they're not stupid. And you're paranoid. Yeah. That's what I think –

JOHN. Yeah, be convenient that, wouldn't it. He's paranoid. He's a drunk. S'why we can't promote him. What am I to you? Police officer who happens to be black, or a black man who happens to be a / police officer.

CARTER. Stop throwing unwarranted muck around the place. At the end of the day, it's about who's most ready and best suited for the role and right now, / that's just not you.

JOHN. I've earned it Carter, you know I've fucking / earned it!

CARTER. All you're about to earn here is a suspension.

CARTER*'s mobile rings.*

JOHN. What?

CARTER (*answering phone*). Yes?… not now. Give me (*Glances at the time.*) ten minutes… right. (*Puts phone down.*)

JOHN. What did you –

CARTER. It's gone too far. They're going to call you in. Three months' sick leave with counselling. I'm the point of contact.

JOHN *can't believe what he's hearing.*

I'm sorry, I hate having to… but you'd drink Dylan Thomas under the table these days, d'you know that. D'you know that about yourself?

Beat.

Take it. Tell them you're going to take it and sort yourself out. You don't have a choice.

We hear the sound of a heart beating way too fast.

Are you hearing me. Are you hearing me John. John. John?

It beats faster and faster, growing in volume, filling the auditorium…

And we're focused on the mortuary again.

The organs from the body have been removed en bloc and are sitting together on a plastic cutting board now.
SAMUEL *is looking at the blood draining into the sink.*
XIMO *is positioned somewhere, watching the examination of his own inner universe.*

SAMUEL. Pomegranate juice.

ANNA. What?

SAMUEL. The blood. Looks like pomegranate juice.

ANNA. Why does everything remind you of food?

GER. Start with the heart.

ANNA *picks up the heart and takes it to the scales.*

SAMUEL (*competitively*). Three hundred grams.

ANNA. Three ten.

They gather around and watch as the scale reaches a measurement of exactly 310 grams.

GER (*making a note*). Three... ten.

ANNA *smiles sweetly at* SAMUEL *who grimaces back.*

Select your scalpel.

ANNA *selects a scalpel.* GER *gives her a nod and she begins the examination. Silence for a while as she works.*

ANNA. Awful way to go.

SAMUEL. S'there a good way?

ANNA (*knowing full well* SAMUEL *hates dealing with bodies that have been submerged in water*). I dunno. Drowning?

SAMUEL. Oh, don't... an' it's not like anyone's ever come back from drowning to tell us what it's like is it, so how the hell do we know.

ANNA (*enjoying this*). Remember that one a few months back? From the / canal?

GER. Anna could you focus on what you're doing please.

ANNA. Sorry.

SAMUEL. Christ. The smell off 'em. (*Makes a face.*) All slippy and swollen with the skin comin' off. Impossible to get onto the table too. Nah. Gimme a straight-up murder any day –

GER. Sam, could you just... (*Gesturing for him to shut up, then selecting a smaller scalpel and handing to* ANNA.) Try this one and go in at an angle like that.

Silence as she works. Then GER *notices that* SAMUEL's *gone a bit pale.*

You alright?

SAMUEL. Huh? Yeah.

GER. You sure?

SAMUEL. Yeah.

Beat.

GER. Shit. Anna.

GER *catches* SAMUEL *as he falls.* ANNA *downs tools to help. He comes to almost straight away, disoriented.*

SAMUEL. Oh my god, what –

ANNA. Did you just faint?

SAMUEL. / What? No!

GER. C'mon. Let's get you some air.

SAMUEL. Nah, I'm fine –

GER. No you need to get some air –

ANNA. Did you actually seriously / just faint?

SAMUEL. Shut up man. S'all / your fault anyway

GER. Hold my arm.

ANNA. How's it all / my fault

SAMUEL. 'Cause you brought up the drowned ones didn't you! / I don't like the drowned ones.

GER. / Samuel, hold my arm.

ANNA. D'you know what it probably was, all that talk 'bout food, yeah? 'Cause you're always / banging on about food.

GER. / C'mon would you.

SAMUEL. Oh shut up Anna –

ANNA. You shut up –

GER. Shut up the both of you. Alright?

ANNA/SAMUEL. Sorry.

GER (*to* SAMUEL). Now come on. (*Walks to the door with him*.) Go slow.

SAMUEL. Will I get marked down for this?

GER (*to* ANNA). Don't touch anything 'til I get back.

GER *and* SAMUEL *exit, leaving* ANNA *alone for a few moments. Her attention keeps being pulled back to the body. She senses something. As if she might not be alone. She turns around slowly and comes face to face with* XIMO, *who is standing beside his body.*

A strange and bizarre moment as they hold eye contact.

Then a shift.

XIMO *picks up the mortuary instrument resembling hedge shears and we are suddenly in a beautiful garden in an upmarket part of Cape Town.* XIMO *starts tending to a plant with the hedge shears. He's singing.* RAE *is watching him. She's wearing dark sunglasses.*

RAE. What is that?

She has startled him.

Sorry, I… (*Laughs*.) Who did you think it would be?

XIMO. I don't know.

RAE. Are you a nervous person?

XIMO. No. Not usually.

RAE.…

XIMO. The name of the song?

RAE. Yes. Right.

XIMO (*gestures that he can't remember*). I just remember my mother singing it. When we were small.

RAE. A lullaby maybe?

XIMO. Maybe.

RAE. Or was it – did she make it up?

XIMO. I really don't know.

RAE hears something and looks behind her.

RAE. Was that a car? I think it… I think that's him. Shit. (*Looks back to* XIMO.) I like your voice.

She exits. XIMO *watches her leave.*

GER *re-enters. The white light disappears.* XIMO *is back in the mortuary again, observing his own autopsy.*

ANNA. Huh?

GER. What?

ANNA. Sorry, didn't hear what you said?

GER. That's 'cause I didn't say anything.

ANNA. Oh. (*Beat.*) He okay then?

GER. Cup of tea, three sugars, he'll be grand.

Gregorio Allegri's 'Miserere' is playing on the radio as ANNA *works on.*

Had a student few years back who fainted whenever he came near the room. Took me a month just to get him through the door.

ANNA *works.* GER *observes.*

'Purge me with Hyssop and I shall be clean.'

ANNA. Eh?

GER (*pointing up, referring to the music on the radio*). 'Miserere Mei Deus'.

ANNA. Oh. Right. What's it mean?

GER. Have mercy on me O God. (*As she observes.*)
    'Wash me and I shall be whiter than snow
    Fill me with joy and gladness
    Then the bones you have broken shall rejoice.'

(*Beat.*) My daddy used love that one. (*Hollering.*) Sam? Still with us?

SAMUEL (*offstage*). Yeah. Two minutes.

ANNA *works on.*

ANNA. This is a bit god-like isn't it? Exploring a per–… nevermind.

GER. Exploring what?

ANNA. Nah, feel stupid saying it.

GER. Go on.

Beat.

ANNA. Exploring a person's like… inner universe.

GER.…

ANNA. I know, sounds really stupid doesn't it.

GER. They're shells now Anna, y'know? That's the way you need to think.

ANNA. Shells?

GER. That's the way you need to look at it.

ANNA. But… where do they end then? I mean, where does a person begin and end and when'd they stop being a person?

A phone starts ringing somewhere.

GER. You need to quit that.

ANNA. What?

GER. That. Whatever that was, needs to – (*Gestures stop.*) Sam, the phone? (*Beat.*) Sam? (*The sound of utensils offstage, clattering as they fall to the floor.*) Christ, has he… Down tools again.

ANNA. Oh for –

GER (*as she exits*). I said down tools!

ANNA. Okay, okay, they're down.

GER *exits calling for* SAMUEL. ANNA *looks at* XIMO's *face again for a moment.*

(*To herself.*) Get a fucking grip Anna.

More time passes in the mortuary. We might hear radio static and fragments of XIMO's *voice dipping in and out.* GER *is trying to tune the radio now while* ANNA *and* SAMUEL *are in the middle of labelling and preparing screw-top containers for toxicology samples.*

Happens all the time actually.

SAMUEL. What, people reversing over their own pets.

ANNA. Yes! If it's small enough and you're not looking properly, course he didn't do it on purpose. (*Continuing the story.*) So anyway, my uncle has to ring up all my cousins, there's five of 'em, so he rings them up one by one and they all want to see her one last time, y'know, before she gets put in a hole out the back garden. But two of them were in Scotland and one was in Skegness, so my uncle says to himself, 'right', and off he goes, vacuum-packs the cat an' sticks her in the freezer with the frozen peas.

SAMUEL. Your uncle vacuum-packed a dead cat an' stuck it in a freezer?

ANNA (*indicating the body*). We put them in fridges, don't we.

SAMUEL. Fucking weirdo.

ANNA. Shut up, Fainty-McFaint.

SAMUEL *gives her the finger.*

GER (*managing to get a station*). Right. Let's crack on with toxicology 'cause if they call here one more time I'll throw the bloody phone through the window. First step Anna?

ANNA. Incision here near the groin area. Then massage the legs to pump the blood up.

GER. Off you go.

They all work on.

ANNA. First time, I couldn't eat bolognese for a month but now I don't even smell it any more, y'know? Or like… less of it anyway.

GER. That's your gag reflexes subsiding. Get used to just about anything in this life.

SAMUEL. Had to have two showers when I got home last night.

GER. Some nights you'll need ten.

They work on for a bit, ANNA *taking blood samples and handing each container to* SAMUEL, *who stores them somewhere ready for collection.*

ANNA. Ever seen one like this before?

GER. Only once. They're pretty rare. He was from Lagos, I think, years back now. Face down in a field outside Gatwick.

SAMUEL. Jesus.

GER. Yep. Snowing that day and there were no tracks leading to or from the body so it was pretty obvious.

A strange sound comes from the radio suddenly. Static mixed with what appears to be a strong wind blowing. Then voices tune in and out, speaking in foreign languages.

ANNA. What the…

They listen for a moment.

SAMUEL. S'that even English?

ANNA. Weird.

GER. One of you drop this?

ANNA. No.

SAMUEL. Didn't touch it.

GER *tries to retune the radio. Sounds distort further and increase in volume. We hear an argument between two people now, someone being slapped and glass smashing.*

The distortion fades and RAE *is revealed, clearing up some broken glass from the floor of a high-end kitchen. She looks like she's been crying. Sinatra's 'Fly Me to the Moon' is playing somewhere and we can also hear the sound of cicadas.* RAE *sees* XIMO *standing in the doorway.*

XIMO. I heard a noise –

RAE. I didn't do this. I don't… I can control my temper, y'know?

XIMO (*going to help*). I know.

RAE. Be careful. It's sharp.

They clear glass for a few moments.

You're up late.

XIMO. Can't sleep.

RAE. Would you like a drink?

XIMO *isn't sure he should.*

Oh c'mon. Have one little drink with me.

XIMO. Are you okay?

RAE. Do I bloody look okay? (*Beat.*) Sorry. Sorry Ximo, I'm not my/self –

XIMO. It's okay –

RAE. I'm just not myself right now.

They continue clearing away glass. XIMO *sees she is desperate for some company.*

XIMO. Okay then, let's have a drink.

RAE. Yes?

XIMO. Why not.

RAE (*pouring out two glasses of whiskey*). All you can do sometimes, heh?

She hands XIMO *his glass.*

Don't you love his voice. Can't sing a note, me. And the irony is I always wanted to be a singer. So really, I'm just a very big disappointment to myself. Cheers.

They clink glasses and drink. She notices his wrist.

What's this. A bird?

XIMO. Butterfly.

RAE. Butterfly?

XIMO (*pointing at the tattoo*). Past. Present. And Future. Transformation. Life is short. Death, certain.

They look at each other for a long moment.

RAE. I'm cold. Are you cold.

XIMO. No, but… (*Starts removing his hoodie.*)

RAE. No, you don't need to do that –

XIMO. It's fine. I'm not cold. Go on, take it.

She pulls on the hoodie. It is the same grey hoodie that ANNA and SAMUEL were examining earlier.

RAE (*noticing her finger*). Shit. Blood. See?

She sucks her finger, looks at it.

I hate it here Ximo. I really fucking hate it.

JAN appears, surprising them both.

JAN. Looks like a real jol in here, heh?

XIMO swings around, almost smashing a glass.

Careful. Don't want to break another one.

RAE. Christ Jan, I thought you'd –

JAN. Thought I'd what.

RAE. Gone.

JAN. Well I came back. (*Looks at* XIMO.) Got something to say?

XIMO. What? No, I –

JAN. Sure about that Kaffir?

RAE. Don't call him that.

JAN. What should I call him then. My bru, eh? My friend?
What the fuck should I call him?

XIMO. Sir please, / just

JAN. Shut the fuck up Kaffir, you / piece of shit

RAE. Don't talk to him like –

JAN. You too, or I swear… I swear.

Silence.

(*To* XIMO *as he goes to a fridge and retrieves a beer.*)
Sitting here in my kitchen with my wife drinking my
whiskey? (*Laughs.*) Who the fuck do you think you are?
Who the fuck do you think *I* am? (*Opening his beer.*) This
country, man, this country's like dry tinder. Matches lying
about everywhere, you understand? (*Drinks his beer.*) Know
what they're doing to migrant Kaffirs like you in the
townships? Opening your chests in broad daylight. Leaving
you to die like dogs in the dirt. Dousing you in petrol just to
be sure. First your problem was us whites. Now it's other
blacks. But you know what your problem has been all along?
You. Just / you.

RAE. You're drunk Jan.

JAN. Shut up.

XIMO *is extremely uncomfortable.*

RAE. You're drunk.

JAN. And you're a whore. A fucking Kaffir's whore.

Pause. RAE *plucks up the courage to fire at him again. This
is a very dangerous game she's playing.*

RAE. Oh to hell with you, you know that? To hell with you!

She exits quickly.

JAN. Come back here. (*Yelling.*) I said come back!

RAE *doesn't return.* XIMO *is frozen to the spot.* JAN *looks at him for a long moment.*

You like her.

XIMO. Nothing happened.

JAN. I think you're lying.

JAN *drinks his beer and considers* XIMO.

My mind, heh? My mind lately. I apologise.

JAN *walks to a sideboard and takes out a knife.*

Nice, isn't it. Made by a master cutler. Very expensive. The handle, see? Exotic hardwood imported from Southeast Asia. Platinum blade. Damascus steel finish. Quite something.

JAN *stands there for a long moment, running the blade through his fingers.*

They don't prepare us, do they. For this life.

He exits in the same direction as RAE. XIMO *stands still for a moment, shocked and unsure. Then…*

A transition…

And we're back in the mortuary.

Toxicology samples have been drawn. ANNA *and* SAMUEL *are waiting for* GER*'s approval before they begin bagging up the organs. They will be put back inside the body in the stomach area – all of the organs contained within one single bag. We also see the police station.* JOHN *is clearing out his desk. He finishes and is about to leave when his desk phone rings. He looks around for someone but no one's there. He puts his box down and answers.*

JOHN. DC Kavura… yeah… right… (*Looks at his watch.*) okay, that's fine. I'll get someone down there. Thanks for letting us know.

He puts the phone down and looks at it for a long moment. He makes a decision, picks up his box and exits.

We are solely with the mortuary again.

GER. Good work. Let's start bagging, then on to reconstruction.

ANNA *bags the organs and then starts sewing up the body.* SAMUEL *assists and* GER *observes. Radio reception dips in and out.*

Damn thing. Must be the batteries.

GER *gestures for* SAMUEL *to switch it off. He does so.*

Silence.

SAMUEL. S'it lunchtime yet? I'm starving.

Nobody answers. ANNA *continues sewing.*

Two thousand foot drop through the air?

He whistles. Again, no one says anything.

Hey, y'know that plane shot down over the Ukraine, yeah? You can watch this video online, right? This couple driving past the field and they start filming on a phone? And the guy's like –

GER (*focus still on* ANNA*'s work*). It's just Ukraine now Sam. Using the definitive article is insulting to Ukrainians.

They work on in silence. SAMUEL *goes and tries to retune the radio. We hear a crackly version of 'The Strange Death of John Doe' playing.*

ANNA. D'you ever work in here without one? A radio I mean.

GER. No. Think we're just about done. (*Picks up a camera and makes sure it's ready to go, testing the flash, etc.*) 'The Strange Death of John Doe', eh?

SAMUEL. Huh?

GER. 'The Strange Death of John Doe.' My dad used sing it. (*Singing.*) 'I'll sing you a song and it's not very long it's about a young man who never did wrong.' Dylan ripped it off for 'Man On the Street.' (*Flash*.) Either of you even know who Dylan is?

SAMUEL. Yeah. That guy who can't sing.

GER (*inspecting the face*). More packing here.

ANNA. Here?

GER. Yeah, cheekbones aren't quite right. Just… try to get the rough shape back but you need to mould with your fingers, y'know?

ANNA *adjusts*.

Okay. Stand back a bit.

GER *starts photographing the body. Each time she takes a photo, a blinding flash goes off. She sings another line of the song.*

'Suddenly he died one day and the reasons why no one would say.'

She zooms in on the face.

Flash.

Flash flash flash.

Then the mortuary freezes as XIMO *sits up on the gurney. The song on the radio plays on as he examines his own body. The ugly stitching in his torso; the unfamiliar padding in his face.*

Then a transition happens…

And JOHN *is standing in the mortuary with* ANNA *now. They are looking at the body.*

JOHN (*pointing at hands*). And these?

ANNA. Old scars. Nothing to do with it. His face bore the brunt.

JOHN (*looking at face*). Looks like he's sleeping.

ANNA. Lot of them look like that.

Beat.

JOHN. So what's the verdict then?

ANNA *glances though some notes to remind herself.*

ANNA. Hypoxia. Hypothermia. Possibly some heart activity before he hit the ground.

JOHN. He was alive?

ANNA. Possibly.

JOHN. How much alive?

ANNA. Not much. We just think the heart was still pumping a bit. From the amount of blood, see. Unconsciousness would've kicked in fairly quickly though. On an ascent like that in an unpressurised part of the plane… d'you want me to get it?

JOHN. Hmm?

ANNA. The SIM card.

JOHN. Right. Yeah. Thanks.

ANNA *exits to get the SIM card.* JOHN *stares at the body, leans in to get a better look. He moves around the table for a different perspective and a transition happens. Perhaps* JOHN *finds himself face to face with* XIMO *momentarily, just like* ANNA *did. Then* XIMO *steps into another place. He's with* RAE *now and they are waiting at the reception desk of the Naval Backpackers Hostel; a small, run-down place on the outskirts of Cape Town.* RAE *is wearing dark sunglasses and seems distressed. Sound of traffic and cicadas. It's very late.*

RAE. Why's it taking so long?

XIMO. I don't know.

RAE. Where the hell has he gone?

XIMO. To get you a –

RAE. I know that but why is it taking so long?

XIMO (*facing her*). Listen. It's not central. We're on the outskirts of town. Nobody knows we are here –

RAE. You don't know that. And he might know something.

XIMO. The receptionist?

RAE. Maybe that's why he's taking so long. He might be making a call, he might be… y'know what, forget it. Tell him to just / forget it.

XIMO. He'll be back / in a

RAE. I don't need the goddamn hairdryer Ximo, I just want to go to the room now.

XIMO. You're being paranoid –

RAE. Oh my god, what have we done, what have we done –

XIMO. It's okay.

RAE. No it's not, it's not okay, he's going to find us and kill us. He's going to find us both and kill us!

She goes to exit.

XIMO (*pointing*). He's coming, see? Look. He's here.

A transition and we hear…

AIRPORT SECURITY MAN (*voiceover*). Now. Most important bit. When you reach the plane, you climb up into the wheel well. Do you know where that is?

XIMO'S VOICE (*voiceover*). Yes.

ASM'S VOICE (*voiceover*). Are you sure?

XIMO'S VOICE (*voiceover*). No.

ASM'S VOICE. Christ, the wheel well can be accessed from the tyre. Climb up onto the tyre, okay? There is a bar above the tyre. Step onto the bar. You with me? You sure?

The mortuary lights flicker momentarily just as ANNA *re-enters, startling* JOHN.

ANNA. Sorry, did I… they do that. Ger says it's the electrics.

ANNA *hands him the little plastic bag with the SIM card inside. He holds it up to the light.*

JOHN. Don't know how we missed it.

ANNA. Ger says police don't like searching dead bodies.

JOHN. Ger says a lot, don't he.

ANNA. She.

He looks at the body again.

JOHN. Still alive.

ANNA. Technically. But he wouldn't have known what was happening.

JOHN. Definitely unconscious then?

ANNA. Probably.

JOHN. Probably? Probably ain't definitely. Probably means there's still an element of doubt.

Beat.

ANNA. Yeah.

Time passes.

Evening. JOHN is sitting at a bar. A jukebox is playing Little Walter's 'My Babe'. We see him inserting the SIM card that ANNA gave him into a mobile phone. He does so cautiously, aware of who is around him. He starts checking for numbers and texts. He presses redial and the last dialled number is automatically punched out. It's an international dial-tone. He waits for someone to pick up.

Then...

A shadowy back room of a betting shop in Maputo, Mozambique. A board game is laid out on the table. A fan whirrs. A police hat sits on the desk. We hear voices outside speaking in Portuguese. Someone laughs loudly. Voices rise. Someone laughs again. Then the door opens and the DOCUMENT DOCTOR *enters.*

DOCUMENT DOCTOR (*to someone outside the room*). Entrar, entrar!

XIMO *enters and stands there awkwardly, while*
DOCUMENT DOCTOR *sits.*

Why do you stand there like that? Sit. Sit!

XIMO *sits while the* DOCUMENT DOCTOR *gestures to board game.*

This game. All night we play this game. But. I am winning. So it is okay. You play?

XIMO. This?

DOCUMENT DOCTOR. Yes. You play?

XIMO. I think. Once, long time ago –

DOCUMENT DOCTOR. Ah! You either play or do not play, there is no in between. See here – (*Pointing to one side of the board.*) this is my board. My side. And I have captured many pieces. So, I am winning. That pleases me for the objective is to win. No? You must play to win.

XIMO. You leave the board on its own like this?

DOCUMENT DOCTOR. What?

XIMO. You… leave the board on its own?

DOCUMENT DOCTOR. What are you implying?

XIMO. I… I / just

DOCUMENT DOCTOR. You mean to suggest that I cheat?

XIMO. I was just making an / observa–

DOCUMENT DOCTOR. I do not cheat! How dare you! Get out!

XIMO. But –

DOCUMENT DOCTOR. Get out!

XIMO *stands.*

(*Laughing.*) Sit. Sit back down. A joke! I am joking.

XIMO *sits back down.*

I like a joke from time to time. Well then my friend. What can I do for you on this fine Maputo day.

XIMO. I need to… I need to get to Europe.

DOCUMENT DOCTOR. Europe? (*Beat.*) That great little continent.

XIMO. They say you can help. They say you are the Document Doctor.

DOCUMENT DOCTOR. Is that what they say?

XIMO. I can pay.

DOCUMENT DOCTOR (*pleased with this title*). The Document Doctor.

XIMO. I have money.

DOCUMENT DOCTOR. I once went to Italy. Lake Como. Lake Como is in the north. You know it? Splendid lake. Just splendid. But. When it rains, it pours! I was in a boat out on that lake when it rained. The heavens above just opened up, and it rained down hard. My shirt was stuck to my chest and my back. (*Beat.*) London?

XIMO. Berlin.

DOCUMENT DOCTOR. Berlin? But if you go to London you can visit the Queen!

XIMO. Well I need to get to –

DOCUMENT DOCTOR. And maybe she will offer you some tea. And little white sandwiches with thin slices of cucumber –

XIMO. I don't like cucumber –

DOCUMENT DOCTOR. Or. Maybe she will kick you in the ass. (*Laughs loudly.*) Hmmm? Maybe she will do that instead. You would prefer the sandwich now, yes?

DOCUMENT DOCTOR *considers him for a few moments. Then he writes out his fee on a slip of paper and pushes it across the table to* XIMO.

The going rate.

XIMO *reads it, then looks at him.*

XIMO. You think I have this kind of money?

DOCUMENT DOCTOR. To the Europeans, that – (*Points to the piece of paper.*) is nothing. You want to go to Europe, no?

XIMO. I don't have this kind of money.

DOCUMENT DOCTOR. Then I can't help you.

XIMO. This is double what I thought it would be.

DOCUMENT DOCTOR. Then leave and stop wasting my time. (*Beat.*) Go!

XIMO. Here. (*Reaches down and pulls out a roll of money tied with an elastic band from inside his sock. He places it on the table.*) That's it. That's everything.

DOCUMENT DOCTOR *unwinds the elastic band and counts out the notes. He notices* XIMO'*s watch.*

DOCUMENT DOCTOR. Nice watch.

XIMO. No.

DOCUMENT DOCTOR. The watch too and we have a deal –

XIMO. I said no.

DOCUMENT DOCTOR. Looks like it tells the time / well.

XIMO. You can't have this watch.

XIMO *starts gathering up his money.* DOCUMENT DOCTOR *leans back in his chair and considers him.*

DOCUMENT DOCTOR. Which animal do you think you are?

XIMO. What?

DOCUMENT DOCTOR. If you were an animal, which one would you be? A buffalo perhaps? Or a mighty elephant? A tiger? Lion? Which animal is yours? It's a test, see? If you give me the right answer, then I'll help you. But if you answer incorrectly – (*Opens out his arms to gesture 'nothing more I can do for you'*.)

XIMO. A test?

DOCUMENT DOCTOR. Just like this life.

XIMO *thinks for a long moment*

XIMO (*quietly*). A butterfly.

DOCUMENT DOCTO (*leaning in*). Excuse me? I couldn't quite…

XIMO. I said, a butterfly.

DOCUMENT DOCTOR. You mean… like a…

He uses his hands to imitate the flapping wings of a butterfly. XIMO *nods.* DOCUMENT DOCTOR *laughs out loud.*

A butterfly? A little butterfly? Ha! A little butterfly that goes flap flap flap. Oh my lord. (*Beat.*) Alright.

XIMO. What?

DOCUMENT DOCTOR. You've passed! I must help you fly away quick before you are squished! So give me all you have, then flap your wings and go visit the Queen.

XIMO *hands the money back over. He reaches into his pockets and finds a few coins which he also places on the table.* DOCUMENT DOCTOR *throws one back to* XIMO.

Passport photos. Go now. I have other work to do.

XIMO. Thank you.

DOCUMENT DOCTOR. Go. I'm a busy man.

XIMO *exits.* DOCUMENT DOCTOR *calls after him.*

Though really, a butterfly isn't even an animal, it's an insect! So perhaps I should fail you after all!

The DOCUMENT DOCTOR *moves a piece on the board. We are not sure if it's his piece, or that of his opponent.*

(*To himself.*) Flap flap flap little butterfly.

The shadowy back room disappears and we're back with
JOHN *at the bar. Another song comes on the jukebox. Maybe*
some Miles Davis. One of the morticians has become a
silent, unforthcoming BARTENDER *who just wants to be*
done for the night.

JOHN (*to the* BARTENDER). O'Gorman got it.

BARTENDER *polishes a glass.*

Gormless O'Gorman.

BARTENDER *continues polishing.*

Gormless O'Gorman got *my* promotion and I got three
months' sick leave? What a fucking day.

BARTENDER *finishes polishing the glass, puts it back and*
starts polishing another. JOHN *drinks.*

(*Half to himself, half to the* BARTENDER.) Three months'
sick leave with counselling handed down directly from top
management. (*Laughs.*) I'm fucked. An' d'you know what I
think? I think he fucking snitched to management to *get* my
promotion, that's what I think. But who gives a shit 'bout
what I think, eh?

BARTENDER *is still polishing.*

(*To* BARTENDER.) Mate, it's clean. The glass? (*Beat.*) Why
aren't you saying anything? Christ's sake, say something,
will you?

BARTENDER *keeps polishing.* JOHN *stares at him.*

Fuck it. Glenfiddich, straight up.

Blackout.

Time passes.

A phone ringing.

A really bright light…

Then chairs stacked on tables – it's closing time but JOHN*'s hanging back, mobile to his ear, waiting for someone to answer, half-empty bottle of Glenfiddich in front of him.*

We see RAE *too. She is at a desk working late. One small light illuminates her work space. There is a cup of tea perched on top of some files. There should be a very distinct difference between the woman we see now and the woman we saw previously. She seems closer to herself somehow; much less out of place.*

JOHN *picks up his coat with his free hand and is about to hang up when:*

RAE. Hello?

JOHN. Hello?

Beat.

RAE. Who is this?

JOHN. Sorry, you... I wasn't expecting anyone to / answer.

RAE. Why do you keep calling? I don't recognise this number and I don't answer calls from numbers I don't recognise, but you just keep calling and calling –

JOHN. Let me... I'm an officer. I work for the Met Police.

RAE. The police?

JOHN. Here in London, that's right.

RAE. London?

JOHN. Yeah. Sorry, where are you?

RAE. Berlin. Look, is this something to do with the Schneider case?

JOHN. What? No. No, that's not –

RAE. Christ. You people have no shame.

JOHN. Sorry?

RAE. Then it's a scam, isn't it?

JOHN. No. No, it's not a scam –

RAE. I'm not giving you any bank details.

JOHN. I don't want your… Just let me explain. Okay? Please?

Beat.

RAE. Go on then.

Partly because he wants to have the rest of this conversation in private, and partly because the BARTENDER *looks like he's about to strangle him,* JOHN *exits. We see only* RAE *now. And perhaps* XIMO. *Maybe he's in the room with her, standing right beside her desk.*

Yes. (*Pause.*) Yes. (*Pause.*) What? (*Accidentally knocks the tea over.*) Shit. Yes, I'm still here, I just… Wait one moment please. (*Covers the mouthpiece of the phone and stares straight ahead, eyes wide. The tea runs all over her paperwork and drips onto the floor. She raises the phone to her ear again.*) I knocked over some tea. It's all over my desk, my notes, my… Is there a tattoo on the left wrist? A small tattoo of a – (*Beat.*) Yes. (*Beat.*) Rudimentary. That's right. (*Pause.*) His name was Ximo. He worked for me in Cape Town. I don't live there any more, it was… it was a long time ago now. He took care of the garden.

RAE's *light fades and* XIMO *finds himself in a busy, sweaty bar in central Maputo. A live reggae band is playing. Crowd dancing. Lights flashing. He scans the crowd, then sees* DOCUMENT DOCTOR, *who is wearing a half-mask with his arms around a woman, also masked, swaying in time with the music.* XIMO *approaches him.*

XIMO. Doctor?

DOCUMENT DOCTOR. Who?

XIMO. Is that you?

DOCUMENT DOCTOR (*raising his mask*). Eh?

XIMO. I've got them. The passport photos.

DOCUMENT DOCTOR (*to woman*). Fique aqui meu amor.

He pulls XIMO *over to a slightly quieter corner.*

You hear that? One of my favourite bands. Live. In this place, tonight. Why you think you can come to me like this.

XIMO. I –

DOCUMENT DOCTOR. Calling me 'Doctor'. I am trying to relax! You think I don't need to chill? You think I should just work ALL DAY LONG?

XIMO. I'm sorry, I / just

DOCUMENT DOCTOR (*laughing*). Relax! Look at your face. So nervous. (*Pats him on the cheek.*) Don't you remember that I like a little joke?

XIMO (*pulling out an envelope*). I wanted to / give you

DOCUMENT DOCTOR (*pushing the envelope away*). Handing me brown-paper envelopes here in front of all these people, are you mad?

XIMO. Of course, I'm / sorry, I

DOCUMENT DOCTOR. I am not joking now. Come.

XIMO *follows* DOCUMENT DOCTOR *outside.*

Outside the club now. We can still hear the muffled music coming from inside. Sound of cicadas, traffic and maybe a few dogs barking.

The walls have eyes here, understand?

XIMO *nods.*

Cigarro?

XIMO *nods again.* DOCUMENT DOCTOR *gives him a cigarette, puts one in his own mouth, lights it, then lights* XIMO's.

I've had a tough day. Had to break up another demonstration. Why do they waste my time like this? Do they really think the architects of Mozambique's illegal debts will crawl out from under their rocks and say 'yes, it was me' because they stand there with placards and looks of defiance on their shit whore faces? (*Takes a long drag.*) Troublemakers, all of them. I have no time for troublemakers.

He gestures for XIMO *to hand him the envelope.* DOCUMENT DOCTOR *opens it and looks at the photos. Looks at* XIMO, *then back at the photos again.*

Most people look like criminals in these, but you? You look sincere. In fact, you look like me when I was your age. Hah! (*Beat.*) So. We meet again in two days and I give you what you want.

XIMO. Thank you.

DOCUMENT DOCTOR. Then you can be on your way. Off to meet your destiny, eh? Do you like my mask?

XIMO. I…

DOCUMENT DOCTOR (*pulling mask down*). Do you like my mask?

XIMO. It's very nice.

DOCUMENT DOCTOR. We're having a fancy-dress party. For my nephew. He has just got a job in the police. We are very happy for him. They say we are a corrupt institution but maybe if they paid us more. Hmmm? (*Holding up envelope.*) A necessary part of life. (*Grabbing him around the shoulders.*) We, we are all brothers, you know? Comrades! You give me what I want, I take care of you. Like a parent does a child. That is our way.

XIMO. So… two days?

DOCUMENT DOCTOR. Is that what I said?

XIMO. Yes.

DOCUMENT DOCTOR. Well then. Now –

He pockets the envelope. The music coming from inside has changed.

I must go. The karaoke is starting. Invented by a very clever Japanese man, you know? Saw the potential in the market.

We hear the mic'd voice of the woman coming from inside, singing badly to the tune of some well-known song.

Oh lord. They will throw things at her. Excuse me.

DOCUMENT DOCTOR *exits.*

(*Calling as he leaves.*) Like a parent does a child!

XIMO (*calling back*). Where should we meet? Here? Doctor? Where should we meet?

Time passes everywhere now except for XIMO*'s time. He remains stationary. Stuck. Unable to move forward or move back. Frozen as the world swirls around him…*

Then a series of images…

GER, *in the mortuary, looking at the SIM card.*
JOHN, *in the mortuary, looking at* XIMO*'s eviscerated organs.*
CARTER, *at her desk, worrying about* JOHN.
RAE, *hunched over, covering her bruised face.*
JAN, *holding a knife.*
DOCUMENT DOCTOR, *looking at* XIMO*'s passport photos.*

We hear XIMO*'s voice, Sinatra's 'Fly Me to the Moon', planes taking off. It's all mixed up together. Off-kilter, distorted. In slow motion.*

Then a MORTICIAN *enters to the sound of a heart beating loudly as he hands* JOHN *a travel bag…*

And we're suddenly in a busy airport. An announcement:

TANNOY (*voice-over*). This is the final call for flight BA984 to Berlin. Please proceed immediately to gate 25. Final call BA 984 to Berlin

A beat.

Then JOHN *walks swiftly through the boarding gate.*

Interval.

A couple of weeks later. The mortuary.

GER. Anna?

ANNA. Hmm?

GER. There's a police officer waiting. Wants to talk.

ANNA. What? Why?

GER. Something to do with that John Doe case a few weeks back. About that SIM card you found.

ANNA. But I gave it to the officer guy.

GER. Don't worry, you didn't do anything wrong, she just needs to talk to you.

GER *beckons* CARTER *in.* GER *then exits, giving them some privacy.*

ANNA. I in trouble or something?

CARTER. I just need to talk to you. Take a seat.

CARTER *takes out a notebook. She makes notes as* ANNA *speaks.*

So you were the one who dealt with DS Kavura when he came to the mortuary that day?

ANNA. Few weeks ago now, yeah.

CARTER. What time was that roughly?

ANNA. Late afternoon I think. Three, four maybe.

CARTER. Was he here long?

ANNA. Twenty minutes or so.

CARTER. Anyone else with him?

ANNA. No. He had ID so I gave him the SIM card. He done something?

CARTER. The SIM card?

ANNA. Yeah, the one found with the body during the external. There was a tear inside the lining of the jeans. He not tell you?

CARTER. Was it locked?

ANNA. Was what locked?

CARTER. The SIM card.

ANNA. No idea. I just bagged it up and got on with the examination.

CARTER. You give him anything else?

ANNA. No. Just the SIM card. In a little plastic bag.

CARTER. D'you remember anything else?

ANNA. Like what?

CARTER. Like… his behaviour. How was his behaviour to you?

ANNA *thinks for a moment.*

ANNA. Seemed a bit shocked when I told him he might've been alive on the way down. Unconscious but… though no one can ever really say for sure can they 'cause we're not them but… yeah. Seemed a bit taken aback by that.

CARTER *makes a note.*

We'd just finished him that morning. Took a while to get the cheekbones right. (*Pointing.*) Still here, fridge number five.

CARTER *puts her notebook away and takes out her phone.*

You sure I'm not in trouble?

CARTER. No. But we will need you at the inquest now.

ANNA. Ger does all the inquests.

CARTER. I'll be in touch.

ANNA. Have I got him in trouble?

CARTER (*phone to ear as she exits*). Hi, yeah, put me through to the guv'nor, will you?

ANNA *watches her leave.* GER *pops her head in.*

GER. You alright?

ANNA. Yeah. Think so.

Beat.

GER. Let's take twenty.

A sudden loud banging from one of the fridge doors as a shift happens. One of the morticians opens the door to reveal XIMO *with a red rucksack on his back. He walks through as if he's walking into the bar where we last saw him with the* DOCUMENT DOCTOR. *Maybe there are echoes of the same music playing and* DOCUMENT DOCTOR's voice – 'flap, flap, flap little butterfly'.*

We should have the sense that it's late and everything is closed up.

He takes out a mobile and checks for texts. Nothing. He looks at the watch.

XIMO. Why so late.

He kicks at some litter on the ground.

(*Shouting out.*) You're late Doctor! You hear me?

A dog barks outside somewhere. XIMO *peers out into the darkness, as if he sees something*

Doctor?

The dog stops barking. Nothing.

He takes out his mobile again and dials a number:

AUTOMATED SERVICE. This number is not recognised. Please check the number and try again.

XIMO *looks at the phone for a moment. He dials again. Again, we hear the automated service:*

This number is not recognised. Please check the number and try again.

He frantically searches his pockets for a piece of paper. He checks the number on his mobile with the number on the piece of paper. He dials in the number carefully. Again:

This number is not recognised. / Please check the number and try again

XIMO. FUCK FUCK FUCK.

Dog starts barking.

Shut up you stupid dog! Shut up!

Dog keeps barking. XIMO *squats and holds his head in his hands. He stays like that for a long moment, inhaling and exhaling deeply. Dog stops barking.* XIMO *makes a decision and starts to walk.*

We see JOHN *now. He's sitting in a small cafe near Littenstraße in the central Berlin locality of Mitte.* RAE *sits opposite him.*

JOHN. Got off at Checkpoint Charlie. Walked from there. Never been, see. Thought I might as well try to catch some of the sights. (*Beat.*) So you're an interpreter then?

RAE. For the courts and notaries here in Berlin. Hearings, trials, that sort of thing. My mother's German. I don't have long.

JOHN. Right.

RAE. May I see it?

It starts to rain outside. JOHN *removes an A4 envelope from his jacket. He takes out a photo and shows it to her. She looks at it for a long moment. Her face is hard to read. Then she nods.*

JOHN. This is the man who worked for you in Cape Town?

RAE. His face looks a little different but... these scars on the back of his hand, I remember them. And this. I know this tattoo. (*Beat*.) The Japanese think they're the souls of the dead.

JOHN. Sorry?

RAE. Butterflies. If one flies into your room it's the spirits coming to pay you a visit.

JOHN *takes the photo back*.

He wasn't with us very long.

JOHN. Was he working there illegally?

RAE. That's not unusual.

JOHN. And you don't have a home address?

RAE. A little fishing village somewhere in Mozambique, that's all I remember.

JOHN. What else d'you know about him?

RAE. I don't really trust the police.

JOHN. Neither do I.

Beat. RAE *doesn't quite know how to respond*.

RAE. He had a brother. Lives in one of the shanty towns in Maputo.

JOHN. Right. Sorry, can I just ask... why'd you leave Cape Town?

RAE. I feel like I'm defending myself here, why do I feel like that?

JOHN. I don't know, it's just a question –

RAE. My marriage broke down, okay? Alright?

JOHN. Sorry to hear that. (*Beat*.) I hope things are working out for you here?

RAE. I'm getting on with my life. And I don't... it's hard for me to go back to that place, that time. Okay? It was a very difficult period. I… I was a mess. But it's in the past now. And I want to leave it there.

Pause.

JOHN. The SIM card. The one with your number, your number here in Germany, that SIM card was from Zambia. But we know he got on the plane in Angola –

RAE. Can you excuse me a moment.

JOHN.…

RAE. I'm not going to jump out a window or anything, I just need the bathroom.

She exits. JOHN *waits, sipping at his coffee.*

In the bathroom, RAE *splashes her face with cold water. Trying to forget. She looks in the mirror and sees something now. A dingy room in the Naval Backpackers Hostel. Herself, sitting on a bed. A car backfires outside. A toilet flushes.* XIMO *enters from the bathroom.*

XIMO. I'll go ask.

RAE. I told you. It's fine.

XIMO. But they've made a mistake, we –

RAE. It's just for one night Ximo.

XIMO *sits on a chair.*

XIMO. At least he found the hairdryer.

RAE. Doesn't work.

Beat.

They laugh.

Is it still terrible? (*Taking off her sunglasses.*) I'm avoiding mirrors.

XIMO *looks.*

XIMO. Yes.

RAE. I like your honesty.

RAE looks about the grotty room.

Cape Town isn't safe for you now. He'll keep looking until he finds you, you do realise that, don't you?

XIMO. I know someone living in Khayelitsha. I'll go there for a while, keep my head down –

RAE. You heard Jan, you know what they're doing to people in the townships. They set fire to a man just last week. He came from Somalia, finally opens his own shop and they set fire to him.

XIMO. I know.

Pause.

RAE. Do you have a birth certificate?

XIMO....

RAE. Do you have a birth / certificate?

XIMO. I don't know, I –

RAE. You don't have one?

XIMO. It might be with my brother in Maputo, but –

RAE. Then go back to Maputo. Find your birth certificate. Come to Berlin. I'm serious. There's work there. I can find you work but you'll need a passport.

Beat.

XIMO. What if I can't find it.

RAE. Then… there are other ways. Angola? You could try Angola. Boats sail all the way to Spain from there. It's a hotspot for that kind of thing, everyone knows it. There are always other ways.

She takes some money out of her wallet and gives it to him.

XIMO. No.

RAE. Take it.

XIMO. I don't expect payment, I didn't do it for mon/ey

RAE. I know you didn't Ximo but just take it. Please. You might need it.

He reluctantly accepts the money.

(*Taking off her watch.*) And this.

XIMO. What?

RAE. This too.

XIMO. No. That's your watch. You like / that watch

RAE (*pushing it into his hand*). Oh for god's sake, if you get stuck, use it. It's just a stupid watch.

XIMO *takes the watch…*

And RAE *re-enters the café area. She sits back down with* JOHN.

JOHN. You okay?

RAE. He was going to Angola via Botswana and Zambia. He called me along the way sometimes. Usually after he'd crossed a border. But the calls stopped a week or so after he made it through to Zambia.

JOHN. Why was he calling you?

RAE. Because I… Because he thought he could find work here.

JOHN. So he was coming here to find you?

RAE. To find work. He thought I could help him find work. It's not uncommon what he was doing.

JOHN. Climbing into the wheel well of a plane is common?

RAE. That's not what I said. I don't know why he did that.

Beat.

JOHN. When was the last time you spoke to him?

RAE. I don't know, a couple of months back maybe?

JOHN. Right. And that was the last time you spoke?

RAE. That was the last time.

JOHN. Can I just ask –

RAE. I don't know why you keep asking me if you can 'just ask' 'cause you'll go right ahead and ask anyway, won't you?

JOHN. Were you in a relationship with him?

Beat.

RAE. No. Look, I really need to get back to work.

JOHN. Anything else you remember? Anything at all?

Beat.

RAE. When he left Cape Town, he went back to Maputo first to find his birth certificate. To try to get a passport. But he couldn't find it. And then some corrupt official stole all his money.

JOHN. So he tried to buy his papers?

RAE *nods*.

Why head for Angola?

RAE. Boats. They sail up along the northwest coast headed for Spain.

RAE *and* JOHN *stare at each other*.

JOHN. But he didn't get a boat, did he –

RAE. Obviously not. Look, are we done here? I don't know what else I can tell you.

JOHN. Why're you so upset? –

RAE. Why do you think?! 'Cause you're all up in my face making me remember things I don't want to remember, showing me photos of dead people, of dead –

JOHN. Alright. Alright. I'm sorry.

RAE *stands up to leave, then hesitates.*

RAE. Felipe. His brother's name is Felipe. Like I said, he lives in a shanty town in Maputo.

JOHN. Where's that?

RAE (*as she leaves*). Maputo, Mozambique. The Chamanculo C, I think. That's all I know.

JOHN. Felipe. Chamanculo C.

They look at each other for a moment.

RAE. If you ever find him, tell him... tell him...

Then she exits abruptly.

A transition. We hear the sounds of a busy airport. An announcement:

TANNOY (*voice-over*). Flight LA302 to Maputo please proceed to gate 28, flight LA 302 to Maputo please proceed to gate 28.

JOHN*'s in an airport lounge in Johannesburg now.*
TRAVELLER *sits beside him reading a travel guidebook.*
JOHN *is drinking a beer.* TRAVELLER *speaks very quickly.*

TRAVELLER. My first time. Very excited.

JOHN. Eh?

TRAVELLER. You're on the same flight, right? Flight – (*Checks ticket.*) LAM 302 to Maputo International Airport?

JOHN. Oh. Yeah.

TRAVELLER. Saw you board in Berlin, you were sat three rows in front of me. Epic journey right? That layover in Qatar was tough. Browsed the magazine section so long they asked me to leave. Least we're on the last leg. I'm meeting some buddies out there for this epic fishing trip we've been planning for, gosh, must be nigh on ten years I guess. Fishing heaven, that's what they say. About Mozambique, I mean. War got in the way there for a while of course, shut the country down but that's all over now. You heard of Black

Marlin? That's what we're after. Talking premiere game
here. Long sharp bills, speeds of up to eighty miles an hour,
hey, you fish?

JOHN. No.

TRAVELLER. I'm always on the lookout for people to chat to
during layovers like this, 'specially if I see them waiting near
my gate.

Pause. TRAVELLER *is waiting eagerly for* JOHN *to say
something.*

Visiting family?

JOHN *just looks at him.*

On your holidays?

JOHN. Why the fuck would you think that?

TRAVELLER. Sorry? / What

JOHN. Why the fuck would you think I'd be visiting family?

TRAVELLER. Jesus mister. Alright –

JOHN. Fuck off and annoy someone else, would ya?

TRAVELLER (*leaving*). Well nice to meet you too.

JOHN. Fucking Americans.

TRAVELLER. I'm Canadian act/ually.

JOHN. Same difference.

We see XIMO. *Still walking. He keeps walking. He just
walks and walks.*

Perhaps we hear snippets of XIMO's *voice.*

Then…

JOHN *and* PAULINO, *a young interpreter, are standing in*
FELIPE's *shack. We should have the sense that* PAULINO *is
enabling* FELIPE *and* JOHN *to understand each other. This
might be through literal translations from Portuguese to*

English, or it might be that FELIPE *and* PAULINO *communicate silently through looks or gestures. Whatever works best for the company.*

Silence.

FELIPE *is looking at the reconstruction photo.*

[FELIPE]

PAULINO. He wants to know how you found him.

JOHN. Luck. In the end. I just kept asking. In the bars, on the streets. Met a girl one night. Said she knew a guy living here whose brother was missing.

[FELIPE]

Why's he smiling like that?

PAULINO. He says, you foreigners like our Mozambican girls, don't you.

[FELIPE]

He says Azungu like you should be careful in places like this.

JOHN. Azungu?

PAULINO. Foreigners.

FELIPE *looks at the photo again and points to something.*

[FELIPE]

PAULINO. He was with him when he had this done. They went to a local master who cut the skin with a sharp blade and then rubbed pigment into the wounds. The blood dried out in the sun.

[FELIPE]

These scars are from their mother. They lost her in the big flood. Ximo tried to hold on for as long as he could.

FELIPE *covers his face with his hands.*

No one knows what to say.

Then he goes and pulls a suitcase out from underneath his bed. He opens it and starts taking out items of clothing.

[FELIPE]

These belonged to his brother. He stored them here. Sometimes, when he had not made contact for a long time, he would open this case like so and take out these clothes. He would lay them on the floor, on the bed, all about the place and then his phone would ring. As if his brother could sense it. Even though he was many miles from home, it was as if he knew his belongings had been disturbed. (*Beat.*) Now he understands why it does not work any more.

Pause.

JOHN. Ask him. If he knows why he did it. Ask him that.

PAULINO translates. FELIPE looks at JOHN, speaking directly to him for the first time.

FELIPE. Because he had a head full of dreams.

Really loud, contemporary African dance music blasts out as a transition takes place. Perhaps PAULINO 'positions' JOHN so he can observe the memory that FELIPE is recalling, as MORTICIANS in the background also become observers, sitting on trolleys to watch while absentmindedly cleaning tools, etc.

FELIPE is on his own in the shack, trying on a pair of white trainers. He finishes tying the laces, then stands up and admires his feet. The case lies open on the floor. XIMO enters and immediately notices the trainers and the case.

XIMO (*turning the music down*). Take them off your stinky feet!

FELIPE. They look better on my feet. Your feet are flat. You have / flat feet.

XIMO. Now Felipe!

FELIPE *begrudgingly starts removing the trainers.*

Stop rooting through my stuff, okay?

FELIPE. Then stop leaving things lying about!

XIMO. Those trainers weren't 'lying about', they were in that case.

FELIPE (*throwing trainers across to him*). Quit whining little brother. Hurts my ears.

XIMO *starts cleaning his trainers.*

Look at you. They've really turned you into a domestic, haven't they. Cleaning that big house with four floors. What did they need four floors for, they didn't even have children! I'd spend the money on a nice car. Maybe a Chevrolet with customised horn. Are you still sulking about those papers? Is that the only reason you came back? Anyway, what you want one of them for? A Mozambican passport is useless, restrictions everywhere you go. Guys like us from the East? We need visas to take a shit. Beer?

XIMO. I don't understand why they were never replaced –

FELIPE. I told you why! Because everything was washed away. Because we were stuck in a tree for two days! (*Grabbing* XIMO*'s scarred hand.*) Because we had just lost our mother. (*Flings his hand away.*) Papers were not on my list of priorities. (*Throws himself into a chair and opens a beer.*) Hey. C'mon now. Tell me again how it happened.

XIMO. I've already told you. I must have told you a million times by now –

FELIPE (*clapping his hands*). Tell me again! I love this story man. So unlike you. Por favor! From the knife bit.

XIMO *sighs.*

(*Getting the ball rolling.*) So he follows her out with the knife…

XIMO. He follows her out with the knife, goes into the
bedroom and locks the door.

FELIPE. Oh man, oh man!

XIMO. I hear her scream. I hear him shout. I shout too and he
threatens to cut off my head and feed it to his dog.

FELIPE. Hehe! But wait for it, 'cause this dog is, this dog is...

BOTH. A miniature Jack Russell!

They laugh.

XIMO. The cat next door would chase this dog up and down the
garden. Up and down, up / and down.

FELIPE (*clapping his hands again*). Go on, go on!

XIMO. So I break down the door.

FELIPE. You break down the door.

XIMO. I wrestle him to the ground

FELIPE. You wrestle him to the ground

XIMO. And I –

FELIPE. And you disarm the fat bastard!

XIMO. He's not fat. Then I threw the knife out / the window

FELIPE. And beat that fat bastard to / a fucking pulp!

XIMO. I told you, he's / not fat.

FELIPE. And then you ...

XIMO. Then I turn and see her. Slumped on the bed. Bloody.
One eye already swelling...

FELIPE *whistles*.

We left that night while he was out cold. Made our way to
the hostel. She got the first flight out.

FELIPE. My brother, the hero.

XIMO. I hate when you grin like that. You look like a madman.

FELIPE. Did you – (*Uses his fingers to indicate sex.*) a lot? When you should have been dusting?

XIMO. Shut up Felipe.

FELIPE. No wonder I haven't seen you for so long. Pop pop pop while the master's away? While the master's away the mouse will play, eh? With master's wife! Did you do it in the swimming pool? I would've done it in his swimming pool. I've always wanted to fuck in a big / blue swimming pool

XIMO. Stop talking about her like that.

FELIPE. Oohoho! (*Beat.*) Crazy naive… what would you do there with her? Will she put you in a suit? Send you to work in the big investment bank with the shiny floors? You don't even speak the language. Forget it! Bad plan. It's you and me now. 'The Sego Brothers.'

XIMO. What are you talking about?

FELIPE. Slum tourism! Come! Come with me. C'mon!

The music blasts out again as another transition happens and FELIPE *and* XIMO *make their way to a lively bar/nightclub. There is dancing, drinking, flirting, people playing pool, etc. You have to shout to be heard.* FELIPE *and* XIMO *continue their conversation…*

(*As he plays pool.*) 'Slum tourism.'

XIMO. Are you drunk?

FELIPE. No I'm not drunk –

XIMO. We don't have a car.

FELIPE. I'll make a deal with Louis.

XIMO. That old goat, his car has no brakes.

FELIPE. His car has brakes –

XIMO. We'd kill all the tourists!

The brothers laugh.

FELIPE. My plan is a good plan!

XIMO. I told you, I don't want to come back to Maputo. Did you take anything else from my case by the way?

FELIPE. No.

XIMO. My good trousers?

FELIPE. Those trousers are shit. (*Observes his brother for a moment.*) So Maputo isn't good enough any more, eh? Not now we've seen how the other half lives.

XIMO. Don't you have some digging to do?

FELIPE. Going to Cape Town to get rich, eh? So where are these riches then? Where? (*Puts a finger to his temple.*) Always dreaming. You should empty that head of those dreams. (*Beat.*) 'The Sego Brothers.' Best guided tours in all of Mozambique! With us, you don't just see beaches and nice cafés. Oh no. With a / Sego Brother tour, you

XIMO. You're talking crazy Felipe –

FELIPE. With a Sego Brother Tour, you get to see all that, AND, for a little extra, a guided tour through the shanty towns of mighty Maputo. Heh?! We don't just give you shops and museums my friend, oh no, that is what we call predictable shit. What we give you is an 'after-dark-gutter-to-the-stars-urban-safari-experience'. Stop and meet the people. Get to know the community. 'The Sego Brothers.' Listen, listen. (*Pretending to read from a leaflet advertising the service*) Included: Driver. That's you. Expert Guide. That's me. Not Included: Lunch. Bring Along: Sun block, camera, rain jacket for the rainy season. Oh, and comfortable shoes. Two hours from start to finish, all for the very reasonable price of one thousand, five hundred Mozambican Meticais. And for an extra three hundred, I sing while we drive. Eh?!

Beat.

XIMO. Expert guide?

FELIPE. You think that's crazy? You want to go to the land of the whites to be like the white man? *That's* crazy. Always flitting about. Flitting from / one place to another.

XIMO. Flitting about? I follow the work! I go where there's / work to be found.

FELIPE. Well go back to Cape Town then! Or Johannesburg –

XIMO. You think I can go back to Cape Town after what happened? You know who he is? Her husband? The connections he has? (*Beat.*) Hey, shouldn't you be at work right now?

FELIPE. Decided to take the day off. In honour of your visit.

XIMO. Have you lost / that job?

FELIPE. I decided to take a / little holiday.

XIMO. You have, haven't you. You've lost your job again! / Dammit Felipe!

FELIPE. I'm tired of digging! My back hurts! Brazilians stealing all our coal. Useless fucking government making useless shitty deals. Letting the Europeans and South Americans walk all over us. So I drink a bit. So what? You want to go to Europe?! You have a home here Ximo!

XIMO. A corrugated iron roof? Stink of rubbish morning, noon and night? A few measly Meticais from some stupid tourist watching us like we're animals in a zoo? No. Do you understand? No. It's like… my chest is full of pressure here. Something pushes from inside out when I am here. Something grips at my heart and squeezes it tight when I. Am Here!

Lights in the mortuary are flickering like crazy. Perhaps some of the MORTICIANS *notice. Then the lights settle again.*

FELIPE. So dramatic. (*Beat.*) You think too much, that's your problem. Have a beer with me. Eh? Cape Town Mafia won't find you here. Have a drink and relax that busy / mind of yours.

XIMO. When you drink you go under. When you go under, I have to support you. I have to look after you then, and I don't know / if I can do it any more.

FELIPE. Family looks out for family. You're family –

XIMO. But who looks out for / me?

FELIPE. What shit has that woman / filled your head with?

XIMO. Slum tourism? 'The Sego / Brothers'?

FELIPE. Why you being like a bushbaby with its tail stuck in a trap. Eh? And I looked out for you. Oh yes I did. When you woke screaming in the night? I'd come put my hand on your forehead. I'd press my hand against your forehead and you would close your eyes. And then I'd sit beside you and wait until your breathing slowed. I looked out for you when I was all you had left. (*Beat.*) In love with the life of the white people? Well let me tell you something little brother. Every morning, they take a nice big shit just like you and me.

XIMO. Felipe?

FELIPE. Yes?

XIMO. You stink of cheap beer.

> FELIPE *laughs a loud sharp laugh, then grabs* XIMO *by the back of the neck and pulls him close.*

FELIPE. Think she cares for you? She used you little brother. She used you.

> XIMO *frees himself.*

> Ah! Enough of this, I'm out of here. Perhaps I'll bump into Prince Harry on the beach and we can eat tiger prawns together, ha? Ha!

> *He goes.* XIMO *stands there for a few moments, then another transition happens as* XIMO *starts to hastily pack up a red rucksack.*

> *We are back in* FELIPE*'s shack with* PAULINO *and* JOHN.

JOHN. So… so he was running then? He was on the run?

PAULINO. You could say that.

JOHN. And there *was* a relationship?

PAULINO (*gesturing to* FELIPE). He thinks so, yes.

JOHN. But that's not… I met this woman, that's not what she told me.

FELIPE. Then she's a liar. (*Beat.*) I want a drink. You want a drink?

JOHN gestures 'no' and PAULINO *exits, presumably to get some drinks.* JOHN *hands* FELIPE *the photos.* FELIPE *studies them for a while. Then looks at* JOHN *for a long moment.*

Thank you John. Thank you.

And it is only in this moment, that JOHN *truly understands what he has brought about.*

Another transition…

The stage becomes a dusty backstreet in Luanda, Angola. Perhaps chairs are tipped over and body sheets from the mortuary draped on top to suggest boat sails. We can hear the sound of the sea. As all this happens, we see XIMO *walking. Walking and walking; snippets of conversations going around in his head:*

'Find your birth certificate. Come to Berlin. I'm serious. There's work there. I can find you work but you'll need a passport.'

'You have a home here Ximo. What shit has that woman filled your head with?'

'A few measly Meticais from some stupid tourist watching us like we're animals in a zoo?'

'Maputo isn't good enough any more, eh? Not now we've seen how the other half lives.'

'My chest is full of pressure here. Something pushes from inside out when I am here.'

'Angola? You could try Angola. Boats sail all the
way to Spain from there. It's a hotspot for that kind
of thing. Everyone knows it. There are always other
ways.'

'You want to go to the land of the whites to be like
the white man?'

And then we are focused solely on XIMO, *trying to drain the*
last few drops of water from a discarded bottle he's just
found. His clothes are dusty and in need of a wash. An older
man, MORUF, *passes by.*

XIMO. Water? Please? Some water?

Beat.

MORUF. Where are you from?

Beat.

I'm not an official.

XIMO. Mozambique.

MORUF. Long way from home. Why have you come here?

XIMO. Someone told me… someone told me once that there
were boats here. Boats that sail to Spain.

MORUF. Not as simple as that my friend. (*Beat.*) How long
have you been travelling?

XIMO. I think… I think almost nine months.

MORUF. And I assume that by now you have run out of
money?

XIMO *nods.*

Can't move forward, can't move back.

Beat.

Come.

XIMO.…

MORUF. Come with me. The good citizens of Luanda have grown tired of this spectacle. They have no pity for your kind here. Not any more.

MORUF *leads the way.* XIMO *follows.*

MORUF*'s simple dwelling.* XIMO *and* MORUF *are both sat at a little table and* XIMO *is eating ravenously. A clock ticks somewhere.*

Where are you going? Algeria?

XIMO. Europe.

MORUF. Paradise then. (*Beat.*) You know someone there? A relative?

XIMO. She lives in Germany. But she's not a relative, she's…

MORUF (*nodding*). So many stories.

XIMO. We haven't spoken for a while, but…

MORUF. More rice?

MORUF *ladles more rice onto* XIMO*'s plate, then sits back and observes his visitor.*

You remind me of myself a long time ago. Begging for water on a dusty street. Lucky for me, I met Oumar.

XIMO. Who's Oumar?

MORUF. An old Malian man with a long white beard. (*Takes out some prayer beads – the same ones we saw the mortuary technicians mistake for a type of necklace.*) These belonged to him. He insisted. For protection, he said. Gave me food, shelter, arranged a place on a cargo van to Algadez. You know of Algadez?

XIMO *shakes his head.*

Very important transit point. Gateway to the Sahara for centuries. Have some cornbread. It's fresh.

XIMO (*taking some bread*). You crossed the Sahara?

MORUF (*remembering*). We even pissed inside the truck such was the need to keep going. (*Gesturing to the ground.*) Bibles. Bones. Strewn about like discarded rubbish. One man looked as if he had died in prayer. Right there, kneeling in the hot sand. Covering his face like this. (*Beat.*) Know what happens when someone is dying from thirst? Their eyes retreat to the back of their sockets and their tongue begins to swell inside their mouth. (*Refilling* XIMO*'s glass with water.*) Dirkou to Dao Timni, across the Libyan border into Tajarhi and eventually Al Gatrun. Hitchhiked to Tripoli, west through Tunisia, Algeria and finally Morocco where I hid in a forest on the outskirts of Melilla for thirteen months. The cornbread, it's good, yes?

XIMO. Thirteen months?

MORUF. Melilla is a tiny village that geographically belongs to Africa but legally belongs to Spain. There were fences of course. And guards with guns. (*Beat.*) So one day, we climbed. Razor wire three metres high but still we climbed. The border guards killed us openly, said we threw rocks. Moroccans blamed the Spanish, the Spanish blamed them back. Nobody was charged. It was then I thought 'enough is enough'. Twenty-seven when I started out, thirty by the time I reached the razor wire. (*Beat.*) Suffering is a school of wisdom my friend. Understand?

Silence.

The clock seems louder.

But if you insist on continuing, then my advice would be to head north to Nigeria. I know someone there who might be able to help. Dead clients are bad for business so he tries his best. He'll take you as far as Libya and from there you can try your luck with the boats. Could stay here a while. I could help you find work in construction. Three, four months, you may have enough to begin your journey.

Silence. The ticking of the clock is unbearably loud now.

XIMO (*to himself*). There must be another way. (*Looks at* MORUF.) There must be another way.

MORUF. There's always another way. Question is, how badly do you want to take it.

XIMO. I can't go back. I've come too far to go back. (*Beat.*) And there's nothing to go back to. Not for me. Not now.

MORUF *nods. Then rises and exits.* XIMO *remains sitting, the reality of his situation sinking in.* MORUF *re-enters with a piece of paper. He hands it to* XIMO.

MORUF. An... acquaintance here, who might be able to... show you another way. Tell him Moruf wants to call in that favour. Tell him that and he'll help.

XIMO *takes the piece of paper.* MORUF *sits back down.*

XIMO. Thank you.

MORUF. Don't thank me because I don't advise it. But. The choice must be yours.

XIMO *folds up the precious piece of paper and puts it in his pocket.* MORUF *looks at* XIMO *for a moment, then pushes the prayer beads across the table towards him.*

Take them. They're yours now. For protection.

A transition, and we see...

The perimeter fence of the Quatro de Fevereiro International Airport, Luanda. AIRPORT SECURITY MAN *and* XIMO *are mid-conversation.* AIRPORT SECURITY MAN *has a torch in one hand.*

AIRPORT SECURITY MAN. Then tuck your legs up like so and stay there. Got it?

XIMO. Got it.

AIRPORT SECURITY MAN (*exhales*). Otherwise you might get crushed.

XIMO....

AIRPORT SECURITY MAN. When the wheels retract. Where do you think the wheels go. Once you're in the air, you can climb into the baggage hold, one of those compartments is pressurised and heated. It's where they put their pets.

XIMO. I can get in there?

AIRPORT SECURITY MAN. Where?

XIMO. Baggage hold?

AIRPORT SECURITY MAN. Yes. I just said that. After take-off.

XIMO. But… which way / do I

AIRPORT SECURITY MAN. Look, it's getting late. We need to move. Do you want to do this or not?

AIRPORT SECURITY MAN *swings around with the torch as if he has heard a noise. He swings back.*

I said d'you want to do this or not?

XIMO. I…

AIRPORT SECURITY MAN. Make up your mind man, I could lose my job here. You either do this, or fuck off home. Now which is it?

Beat. Then XIMO *nods.*

Okay.

Puts out his hand. XIMO *looks at him.*

The watch? You said you had a watch.

XIMO *hesitates.*

Moruf thinks I'm going to risk my job for a few measly kwanza? Get real brother. We had a deal. Now hurry the fuck up.

XIMO *removes the watch and hands it over.*

You can't bring that by the way.

XIMO. What?

AIRPORT SECURITY MAN. That bag. You can't bring it. No room. (*Pointing at the watch face.*) You need to go. Window closes at half-past, remember? (*Pointing.*) The breach in the fence is three hundred yards that way.

AIRPORT SECURITY MAN *goes to exit.*

XIMO (*calling*). Take care of that watch.

AIRPORT SECURITY MAN (*as he exits*). Crazy fuck.

As XIMO *steps through the breach in the fence, the sound of planes becomes very loud.*

He removes the rucksack from his back and takes out his mobile, the spare SIM card and some money. He also takes out the items we saw SAMUEL *and* ANNA *logging in the mortuary at the beginning. The red T-shirt with the green stripes…*

XIMO (*to himself as he puts it on*) Lucky T-shirt.

The white trainers…

(*Putting them on.*) Brand new.

The prayer beads…

(*Kisses them.*) For protection.

XIMO *then puts on the old grey hoodie – the one from the mortuary with the illegible label and the same one he once gave to* RAE *when she was cold. He closes up the rucksack and discards it. He takes a deep breath.*

The sound of planes grows louder and perhaps we hear audio from a cockpit, snippets of XIMO's *voice or snippets from some of the* VOICEMAILS. *Maybe there is also a brief mirror-image here, of the moment we first caught sight of* XIMO *at the very top of the play…*

And we're now outside the Coroner's Court. CARTER *is smoking a quick cigarette before heading in.* JOHN *appears.*

Slightly uncomfortable pause.

CARTER. Dirty habit.

JOHN. Thought you quit?

CARTER. So did I.

She offers him one. He accepts. She lights it for him. They smoke.

How you been John?

JOHN. Alright. Yeah, alright.

CARTER. You look good. (*Beat.*) Tried to come see you. When you first went in but they wouldn't let me.

JOHN. Yeah. They're pretty strict about all that.

Beat.

CARTER. And I know this is stupid but... I've had visions of that film in my head ever since. The one with Jack Nicholson and all them other mad fellas? One about the cuckoo?

JOHN *smiles.*

JOHN. He wasn't mad y'know.

CARTER. Jack Nicholson? Yeah. Yeah, I know.

Beat.

So... what'll you do now? S'there a plan?

JOHN (*shrugging*). Might be moving to Devon. Dunno yet.

CARTER. Devon? I love Devon. I love being by the sea. S'good for the soul. (*Pause.*) Why you here John. I mean, I'm only here 'cause I have to be.

JOHN....

CARTER. Guess you don't need to explain do you. Not any more.

They smoke.

O'Gorman had a meltdown last week. At his desk one minute, next thing he just stands up and walks out. Just like that. Just walks right out. (*Pause.*) Maybe you're the lucky one John. D'you ever think about it like that? That you're the lucky one?

JOHN *studies her for a moment.*

JOHN. You're a good person, but you don't fucking get it.

CARTER. I don't... get what?

JOHN *gathers his response.*

JOHN. Nothing's changed. It's just... adapted. D'you understand me? (*Beat.*) An' I'm tired now. I am so. Fucking. Tired.

CARTER *has no idea how to respond. So she just extinguishes her cigarette and walks into the Coroner's Court.*

Inside the Coroner's Court. Inquest underway. An AVIATION SECURITY OFFICIAL *is in the witness box. Perhaps the* CORONER *is seated at a higher level than everyone else.* JOHN *is watching from the gallery.*

CORONER. So, as someone with considerable knowledge of aviation security, in your view this type of breach could pose significant threats to the broader issue of public health and safety?

AVIATION OFFICIAL. Yes.

CORONER. Can you explain how exactly?

AVIATION OFFICIAL. Really? I have to explain it?

CORONER. If you wouldn't mind.

AVIATION OFFICIAL. If someone can scale a perimeter fence and hide away in the landing-gear retract area of a Boeing jet... I mean, an IED can be as small as a radio transmitter. Did you know that? That size, look?

CORONER. For the benefit of the court, are you talking about an Improvised Explosive Device?

AVIATION OFFICIAL. Potentially being secreted on the aircraft, yes. I'm surprised the industry isn't kicking up more of a fuss about this. I mean, if the airfield itself is porous then – (*Throws up his hands in a gesture of defeat.*) what's the bloody point? Might as well forget about security checks altogether and save ourselves the hassle. And, what if he'd fallen on someone. Like, right on top of someone out walking their dog or something.

***

CARTER *is in the witness box now.*

CARTER. Initially we treated the incident as a possible violent assault. We thought perhaps he'd been struck from behind with a blunt instrument. But we realised pretty quickly that wasn't what we were dealing with.

CORONER. What made you think that?

CARTER. Spread of body matter. Suggested he'd fallen from a height. And every few minutes a plane would pass low overhead so... didn't take a genius.

CORONER. Through phone numbers obtained from a SIM card that was... withheld until quite recently, the court understands that the victim's former employer, currently living in Berlin, knew of his plans to travel to Europe?

CARTER. That's right, yes. He was her gardener for a while when she lived in South Africa.

CORONER. But she did nothing to facilitate his trip?

CARTER. No. He made the journey alone. It was his own undertaking.

CORONER. The court also understands that there's a brother?

CARTER. Yes. In Mozambique. That's where he was originally from. The brother knows about the inquest but can't afford to be here.

CORONER. That's unfortunate.

***

ANNA*'s turn.*

ANNA. They were very severe.

CORONER. Can you describe them in more detail?

ANNA. Ummm… huge amount of damage to the skull and brain. Fractures to the spine and pelvis, broken left arm, right shin was fractured and there were loads of other cuts and bruises on his… on the body. Consistent with a fall from that height.

CORONER. Toxicology tests all clear?

ANNA. Yeah. Yes.

CORONER. And it was you who found the second SIM card?

ANNA. During the external, yeah.

CORONER. And passed it over to DS Kavura?

ANNA. He had ID.

CORONER. I just need a simple yes or no. For the record.

ANNA. I gave the second SIM card to DS Kavura, yeah. Yes. Sorry.

***

GER*'s turn.*

CORONER. Was the victim already dead upon impact with the ground, or was it the impact with the ground that killed him?

GER. We can't be absolutely sure. He may have been alive on impact but almost certainly unconscious.

CORONER. In your opinion, what's the most likely scenario?

GER. In my opinion, he was either extremely close to the point of death or already dead.

CORONER. When he hit the ground?

GER. When he hit the ground.

***

CORONOER*'s verdict.*

CORONER *is looking through some notes; then addresses the room.*

CORONER. Alright then. The forensic evidence and various witness statements heard here this afternoon lead me to conclude that the death of – (*Looks at a piece of paper.*) Joaquim Armando Sego, otherwise known as Ximo, was of an accidental nature. No other persons or institutions appear to have been involved and it seems unlikely that this death could have been prevented. Having listened carefully to the opinions of the expert in aviation security, I do not believe this case highlights a direct threat to the broader issue of public health and safety. Having said that, it is this coroner's recommendation that the relative aviation representatives here work more closely with airports such as the Quatro de Fevereiro International in Luanda, to develop new security strategies that reduce the possibility of an accident like this happening again. As always, a copy of any depositions taken during the inquest as well as a copy of this verdict will be made available to members of the public and any other interested parties.

Beat.

Okay. We're done here. Thank you.

CORONER *collects up notes and exits.*

The Naval Backpackers Hostel again. XIMO *is looking at the watch he's just strapped to his wrist.*

XIMO. You should get some rest. It's an early flight. I'll sleep in the chair.

RAE. No one can sleep properly in a chair.

XIMO. I can.

RAE. You can't.

XIMO. It's fine –

RAE. You don't… I don't want you to do that.

Pause.

I don't.

XIMO *stays where he is.*

A baby starts crying in one of the nearby rooms. Someone shouts from somewhere. The walls are like paper.

This place is a shithole.

XIMO. Close your eyes. Rest.

She reads something scratched into the bedframe. Traces the words with her fingers.

RAE. 'The Mullet. Woz 'Ere.' (*Beat.*) That's a fish. A mullet is a fish.

XIMO. So?

RAE (*sitting up*). A fish in a bed? Sleeping with the fishes? Talk about an om/en!

XIMO. Rae, tell your brain to stop now.

Pause.

RAE *lies back down and tries to sleep.* XIMO *switches out the light.*

Darkness.

RAE. This day. I'll never forget this day.

XIMO. This day is a good day. This day is the start of something new. Something better. Maybe for us both.

Silence.

RAE. Can't sleep.

XIMO. Try.

RAE. I can't.

XIMO. Shall I sing you a lullaby?

RAE *pushes him playfully.*

RAE. Go on then. I like your voice.

XIMO *starts singing gently, his voice soothing the atmosphere. It's the same song we heard him singing in the garden in Cape Town.* RAE *starts to cry.* XIMO *stops singing.*

Lie down.

XIMO *hesitates, then lies down next* RAE.

(*Almost a whisper.*) I won't abandon you. I won't ever abandon you. I swear.

A transition…

It's late evening at the mortuary. Floors have been mopped, storage and fridge areas cleaned, paperwork done. GER *and* ANNA *are sat waiting for the funeral home people to collect* XIMO*'s body for burial.*

ANNA. Sam thinks that the soul is the brain.

GER. How'd he work that one out?

ANNA. So like… he was talking about the brain being like the memory on a computer? 'Cause the memory on the computer's what runs all your programmes? So like… when the computer's switched off the memory's all gone and the machine can't function? So with the brain, the memory's all gone by the time *we* get to it. Obviously. 'Cause we're holding the brain in our hands. So it's the closest thing to the soul 'cause the soul ain't physical just like memory. Therefore, the brain is the closest we can get to a person's soul in his opinion. (*Beat.*) Or maybe he meant something else. I switched off halfway through to be honest.

GER. I feel time.

ANNA.…

GER. When I'm holding a brain in my hands. That's what I feel 'cause that's what we are. Our lives are strung out between birth and death an' all that stuff in the middle? That's time and possibility. We're the possibility of a life and if you want to live, really live, then keep death on the horizon and don't ever take your eyes off it, not even for a second. (*Looks at her watch.*) They're late. Should've been here half an hour ago.

ANNA. I'm not in any rush.

GER. Right then.

GER *exits for a few moments.* ANNA *stares at the body. Then, in* GER*'s absence, she reveals the prayer beads and carefully wraps them around* XIMO*'s wrist.*

A pause.

GER *re-enters with two glasses of whiskey, one of which she hands to* ANNA.

ANNA. We allowed?

GER. Absolutely not. Cheers. And congratulations on passing your diploma. Top marks an' everything. Well done you.

They drink.

ANNA. 'Okay. We're done here. Thank you.'

GER. What did you expect?

ANNA. I dunno. It was just short, wasn't it.

GER. The objective is to establish what happened, record an official verdict, nothing more. (*Beat.*) S'the only thing that ever got to me, y'know. The John Does. The ones left in storage so long the council has to fork out for a funeral that no one even attends.

ANNA. I might. I might go.

Beat.

GER. Well I can't stop you.

They drink.

You know what the best thing is about this job? The power. The power to stand up in court and help the defence close a case or bring an inquest to a conclusion. The power to tell a grieving mother how her son was killed, how long it took him to die and how much pain he was in. They want to know these things and you have the power to tell them. They find comfort in the details, it helps them move on. I find that satisfying, y'know? You're not cutting them open and sewing them back up again for nothing, for no one. You're sending them back to someone who gave a shit and wants answers. But the John Does, well... they feel like hollow little victories to me.

Pause.

ANNA. I get that.

GER. I know. That's why you'll make a very good pathologist. You're a woman. (*Beat.*) Don't tell Sam I said that.

ANNA *notices someone standing in the shadows.*

ANNA. Hello?

GER. Crap, that's not him is it?

JOHN *emerges.*

Oh. Thought you might be... Can I help you?

Pause.

JOHN (*indicating the body on the floor*). Where they taking him?

GER. Twickenham. Lads from the funeral home should be here soon.

JOHN. He should be going home.

GER. Family can't afford it.

Beat.

JOHN. They put 'em in unmarked graves an' wait 'til they fill up, did you know that? (*Beat.*) Took a daytrip down to Lynton last week. S'in Devon. Pretty. By the sea. S'where what's-his-face wrote *Chronicles of Narnia*. There's this place with all these cliffs called Valley of Rocks. Goats up there an' everything. Free-range, big hairy fuckers. (*Beat.*) Went walking up there. Wind was so strong it made my ears hurt but I kept going an' when you reach the top... view worth dying for. Beautiful, y'know? (*Beat.*) Few feet away from me to the left was this bird, right? Hovering above the rocks. Swept off one minute, back again the next. Fighting, see? To get to where the wind didn't want it to go but it never gave up. It never gave up 'cause I guess... I guess it just needed to go that way.

He points to the tattoo.

Looks a bit like a bird, don't it.

ANNA. It's a butterfly.

JOHN. Yeah. They let the blood dry out in the sun.

Beat.

GER. I'm sorry but... I'm going to have to ask you to leave now.

JOHN *nods. Goes, then turns back.*

JOHN. He was trying to get to Berlin, y'know. He wasn't even on the right plane. (*Beat.*) S'cold in here. I'm cold. Are you cold?

GER. You get used to it.

JOHN *exits.*

GER *and* ANNA *just look at each other for a moment.*

ANNA. How'd he get in? Did someone let him in?

GER *has no words. She just raises her eyebrows, shakes her head a bit and finishes her drink.*

A buzzer sounds from outside.

GER (*collecting up the paperwork*). Right. I'm assuming that's them this time.

GER *exits.* ANNA *moves to the end of the gurney and looks at* XIMO. *She touches his foot. A strange and surreal moment as* XIMO *sits up and looks directly at* ANNA...

XIMO. I saw something from the top of a tree once. I was clinging to the top of a tree and night was everywhere. But then lightning came and it all lit up. The world went from black to purple to black again. Flashes of purple lighting up the dark. A tiny flash in the dark.

And I was there.

XIMO *reaches out his arm and* ANNA *touches his hand.*

I was there.

His hand is warm.

I was.

XIMO *lies back down on the gurney.* ANNA *hesitates for a moment, then she goes and touches his heart, checking to see if he is alive. She knows this is crazy but she's compelled to do it anyway.* GER *re-enters and sees this.*

ANNA. Ger?

GER. Yeah?

ANNA. I… ummm… I…

Beat.

GER. Have I told you about lemon juice?

ANNA. What?

GER. Lemon juice. When soap doesn't work? Always does the trick.

Pause.

Then ANNA *steps away from the body, leaving* XIMO *alone.*

Lights in the mortuary suddenly go out.

As the space is plunged into darkness, we hear the sound of a huge flock of birds taking flight. It fills the entire auditorium, the beating wings echoing into silence…

End of Play.

www.nickhernbooks.co.uk

facebook.com/nickhernbooks

twitter.com/nickhernbooks